Poland
Dares
to Speak Up!

Selected Essays
by
Piotr Jaroszyński

Poland
Darcs
to Speak Up!

Dom Polski
Warsaw 2012

Translated from the Polish by Krzysztof Zarzecki,
Hugh McDonald, Paweł Styrna

Text proof-reading: Piotr Szarkowski, Marek Żelazny

Cover Design: Krzysztof Tomaszewski

Interior page design and DTP: Expo Graphic Sp. z o.o.
30-053 Kraków, ul. Kronikarza Galla 1 B /4
tel. +4812/ 631 37 00, fax +4812/ 631 37 07
e-mail: krzysztof.tomaszewski@expographic.com.pl
www.expographic.pl

Illustrations: Author's archive

Cover: Piotr Skarga (1536-1612)
the most famous Polish preacher and prophet

ISBN 978-83-931054-1-0

Published by Dom Polski
03-949 Warszawa, ul. Wandy 14/10
Poland
e-mail: dompolski@piotrjaroszynski.pl
www.piotrjaroszynski.pl

Printed in Poland

Author's Foreword

Sometimes silence is golden. This is so when a rash word of ours may hurt, or even harm someone. It's especially important when we deal with overly sensitive or sick people. It calls for tact and circumspection. We must remain in control of ourselves and hold our tongues. There are also circumstances when we must remain silent in order not to betray an all-important secret. Sometimes this calls for true heroism. In Poland, during and after World War II, oppressors resorted to torture in order to obtain information from the captured soldiers of the underground anti-Nazi, anti-communist resistance army. Some, unable to bear the suffering, betrayed their brothers-in-arms; others, uncertain of their power of endurance, swallowed poison; still others didn't breathe a word under torture and took their secrets to the grave. There are times, situations and challenges when we must remain silent. Whoever does remain silent is then a hero.

However, there are also times when we should not remain silent, indeed we must not! Another imperative comes into force then, which was defined by the ancients: *Qui tacet, consentire videtur* (Whoever remains silent, gives consent). Yes, silence is no longer a mark of heroism then but indeed becomes a mark of outright cowardice. When is it so? First of all, when lies are disseminated in public life, and corruption propagated. We must speak up bravely then. Why bravely? Because such actions may bring serious blows, both verbal and in the form of discrimination. This happens when people who care nothing for moral principles, faith and patriotism, and who will resort to any means to intimidate those who preserve a healthy conscience, have gained the upper hand in both the media and in politics. When intimidation is not sufficient, they will keep slandering the defiant person or, exercising their acquired power, will rely upon various tools of revenge, including terminating that individual's employment.

Nowadays an often ruthless struggle is being waged in Poland. Its aim is to corrupt our Polish consciences, so that we will lose the ability to distinguish a person from an animal, a woman from a man, a wife from a husband, the nation from human resources, subjugation from independence, and ideology from faith. In this struggle, we cannot surrender: we must defend ourselves wisely, we must speak up, we must not keep silent! Silence is consent, and there can be no consent to that which threatens our culture. Most of the essays collected in this volume were initially aired on Radio Maryja and on TV TRWAM, and were published in the weekly magazine *Nasza Polska* and in the daily *Nasz Dziennik*. Some were delivered at the international conferences. I hope they will inspire the readers to further reading and reflection, to discussion and study, because the problems that they probe are of the utmost importance and relevance.

This book is written for everyone but especially for ordinary people who in their everyday lives find deep and troubling issues confronting them in their relationships in their work, or within their families, or just in their lives generally. It tries to look at these and examine them from their point of view, in language and ideas which may give them some understanding about these very issues.

I would like to express my thanks to doctor Antoni Gliwa, Piotr Szarkowski, Krzysztof Tomaszewski, Krystyna Zaremba and Marek Żelazny who were very helpful in preparing this book for publication.

Warsaw, September 17, 2011

Contents

The Treasure of Polish Culture

Poland lies in Central Europe. The Polish state began over a thousand years ago, in the year 966 A.D. to be precise. Poles belong to the Slavic tribes. Over the past one thousand years, the people who lived in Poland created their own culture. This culture has local elements, national elements, and also universal elements that are common to Europe and to the whole world.

Some people are fascinated by other cultures, but other people could not care less. Some people are locked within their own culture, and they regard other cultures with disinterest or even contempt. Others regard mass culture as culture in the primary sense, and they feel no need for a national culture. Others know their own culture and also have a specialized knowledge of others. Finally, there are those who know their own culture and have a lively interest in the treasures of other cultures. These people see that knowledge of other cultures can enrich their own. My personal opinion is that every intelligent person who has reached a certain level of education should be interested in and open to the contributions of other cultures. I know who I am, but I will gladly learn and draw from what is good in others. I know that you have roots in various nations, that you are not all Polish, so I will speak about Polish culture as I would to people who are open to the treasures of a culture other than their own.

First, I will say a few words about what culture is and what a nation is. The word "culture" comes from Latin and it first meant "cultivation". It was first used to mean tilling fields (*agri cultura* or "agriculture"), and then it was used as a metaphor for the cultivation of the soul (*animi cultura*). Cicero used the term *cultura* in this sense. The ancient Greeks already had a term for this – *paideia*. The term "nation" comes from the Latin verb *nascere* – "to be born".

Although this suggests that a nation is based on a common ancestor, the most important thing is that belonging to a particular nation implies belonging to a single culture. A nation is a certain community based on a common heritage that develops one culture over the course of generations. A national culture is the material and spiritual accomplishment and heritage of a certain community.

When we speak of the treasure of Polish culture, we are thinking of the rich heritage that has been developed over generations.

There are four elements in any culture: *theoria, praxis, poiesis,* and *religio. Theoria* includes science and education. *Praxis* includes ethics, economics and politics. *Poiesis* includes craftsmanship, the fine arts, and technology. *Religio* includes faith. A society is civilized in proportion to the development of these domains of culture. They may be developed in different directions and to different degrees, and this will form the character of a civilization. I am not interested here in evaluating various civilizations, to say which is better and which is worse, but I am interested in what a culture has to offer to the people who live in it. Does their civilization give them the opportunity to develop fully as persons, or does it incline them to become vegetables? Perhaps a given culture even does damage to those who live in it. To a large extent, who a person is depends upon the society and culture in which he or she lives in.

Polish culture is the result of the efforts of many generations among whom there were certain outstanding geniuses, and it is truly a treasure for the Poles who are closest to this culture. It was also a treasure for the Slavic peoples who are closely related to Poles at a time when they themselves had not yet achieved the same level of development. It has also been a treasure for the other European nations, especially for the elite who were open to that various forms of higher culture. Polish culture added a certain tone and direction to the development of civilization in general. ˋ

As a state and nation, Poland appears in the historical arena in the second half of the tenth century. The decisive moment was the baptism of Mieszko I, the first historical ruler of Poland, and with this the political status of Poland was recognized in Europe. The various tribes dwelling in Poland were joined to the heritage of Greek, Roman and Christian culture. This baptism had more

10

than a religious meaning. It also meant that Poland was taking its place in the circle of the older Western civilizations. This had an effect on education, science, law, morality, art, and the customs of the Polish people. Latin civilization was the factor that unified the various tribes into one Polish nation. This civilization has been creatively cultivated and preserved over the centuries by the people who live on Polish soil, and this has become the unique culture of Poland.

Now I would like to speak about certain aspects of Polish culture. A nation is not always defined by a unique language. There are many different nations that speak English, and the same goes for Spanish and Portuguese. There are many nations like Switzerland where there are two or more languages. In most cases, however, at least historically, a particular nation has a particular language. When a nation has more than one language, this might be the result of a political union of many nations, as happened in Switzerland. Many nations may speak one language as a consequence of colonial expansion, such as the English and the Spanish. Poles share one language, the Polish language. Mikołaj Rej, one of the first great Polish poets of the sixteenth century notes this with pride when he wrote: "And let the other nations always know / That the Poles [have] not anserinae – they have their own language." This means that Poles do not gabble like geese, but they speak a human language, their own language. For centuries Polish literature developed in the bosom of the older Latin literature. Latin was the common working language of Medieval Europe. Polish documents of that time are in Latin, with the names of Polish people and places appearing sporadically. At the end of the twelfth century, or at the beginning of the thirteenth, someone wrote the beautiful song "Bogurodzica" ("Mother of God"), which was first sung by Polish knights, and today is sung at very special events.

In the fourteenth and fifteenth centuries many verses and songs were penned, both religious and secular. In the sixteenth century two great Polish poets appeared like shining stars, Mikołaj Rej and Jan Kochanowski. Kochanowski was educated in Western Europe and possessed a good knowledge of Latin and Greek, as well as several modern languages. He translated many foreign works into Polish and also wrote poetry in Latin, but eventually he took the great step of writing in Polish for Poles. Let me try to show you an English rendition:

O Muse, let us cast off from the lovely banks of the Tiber...
The peaks of the Carpathians that scrape the sky has long been calling me,
The mountains of my native land have long been calling me,
to their delightful grottos and graceful valleys,
and they order me to sing of the faraway Polish land
with a many-stringed lute in the melodies of my fathers.
I will sing, if I may give glory to Poland with song.
Let my friend Łaski adorn Poland with fat spoils as he wages
war with the Scythians who are bound by no law.
Our hope is in the pen and in the favor of the Muses.
This is my bounty, this is my chariot and sword.

(Elegy 13, Book III)

Kochanowski's language is more refined than the language of Rej. It shows the signs of education and a greater command of language and ideas. His language set the direction for the development of the Polish language. In his own time Jan Kochanowski was recognized throughout Europe as a great poet.

While we are on the topic of the Polish language, we should remember the great work which took place translationing from other languages. Translations have an important role in the life of every nation. They make the accomplishments of other nations accessible to all. When foreign works are available in our own language, they are assimilated into our culture. Translations also have a creative and formative influence on the development of a growing language. It requires a great effort to express things said in a more developed language and at the same time to respect the unique character of the language into which the work is being translated. The work of translators helped the Polish language develop both syntactically and conceptually. The developing language became a means for a broader group of people to enjoy the fruits of ancient classical culture. The Poles were the first among the Slavs to translate classical works, and the other Slavs found that the Polish translations were more available and easier to understand than the original works. As the Polish language developed, it had an important influence on the culture and character of neighboring nations. Aleksander Brückner, one of the leading experts on Polish culture wrote: "The European culture of Poland did not parade itself in a spirit of triumph. In the fifteenth century Russians would satisfy their spiritual hunger with Polish works. They would overlook the difference of creed and the dogmas that contradicted their own. They translated the creatively translated Polish works into their own language, but the translations into Russian were not creative. The translated works used the Russian language and alphabet, but they were interspersed with additions from the Polish language. As early as the fifteenth century we find more and more words and expressions borrowed from Polish in the official texts of Belarus and Lithuania. Later this phenomenon took on monstrous proportions. We find texts that are Russian in form and alphabet, but using Polish thought and vocabulary. Such works are Polish in spirit, content, style and form, while Russian is merely a robe thrown over everything."[1]

He continues: "The material culture was different. That culture reached Moscow directly from England, Holland and France, but the intellectual culture of Poland affected Lithuania and Little Russia, and through them made its way to Moscow, where it reached the court of the Czar and the patriarchs. The result was a rich and varied body of literary works in seventeenth century Moscow which had been translated from Polish."[2]

Poland lost its sovereignty at the end of the eighteenth century. Before the eyes of the world, Poland's neighboring states robbed Poland of its existence as a state, but this did not interrupt the continuity of Polish culture. In a series of annexations, Prussia, Austria and Russia carved up Polish territory among themselves

1. A. Brückner, *Wpływy polskie na Litwie i w Słowiańszczyźnie wschodniej*, [w:] *Polska w kulturze powszechnej [Polish Influence in Lithuania and Eastern Slavic Countries*, (in:) *Poland in Universal Culture]*, ed. F. Koneczny, Cracow 1918, vol. I, p. 162.
2. Ibid., p. 164.

until in 1795 the Polish state ceased to exist. Poland would not regain its sovereignty until 1918. As Pope John Paul II said in an address to the United Nations, it was our culture that enabled us to preserve our spiritual sovereignty. He said: "I am the son of a nation that has survived the most terrible experiences in history. The nation has been condemned to death many times, yet it stayed alive and preserved its identity. It preserved its identity and its sovereignty even during the periods when its land was divided and occupied. The nation could not rely on any other means, such as physical force, to survive. It relied on its culture, and this culture eventually proved to be a greater force than the military and political force of its enemies."[3]

Because of this cultural sovereignty, Poland regained its political independence after one hundred and twenty three years of subjugation. It was during the period of occupation in the nineteenth century that we find the greatest Polish poets. Next to Jan Kochanowski who is regarded as the single greatest, we find the poetic works of Adam Mickiewicz, Juliusz Słowacki, Zygmunt Krasiński and Cyprian Kamil Norwid. We regard them as the seers or prophets of our nation. After them come the great writers of prose: Henryk Sienkiewicz, Bolesław Prus, Władysław Reymont, and Stefan Żeromski. Their Polish speech brought together all the currents of the life of the nation and state. It was recognized throughout Europe and the whole world. The works of Polish authors have been translated and often imitated, and they have won numerous awards, including four Nobel Prizes.

The Polish language achieved a high state of development that enabled writers to express the spirit of the nation in matters both great and small. In our own language we have our own literature of all categories, and the important works of world literature have been translated into Polish as well. Henryk Sienkiewicz even went so far as to say that the Polish language is a special gift of God, a gift that can only be compared perhaps with the Greek language. This is a great treasure of the Poles, which the neighboring Slavic nations would draw upon over the centuries as they began

---

3. UNESCO, 1980.06.02 (14).

to understand and read in Polish. Thanks to Poland, there was something for them to read.

A nation's treasure is found in its wisdom and knowledge, and the propagation of these treasures. Now I would like to mention Polish learning and education.

Polish education began with the acceptance of Christianity. Pagan Poland had no schools. With the Church, soon parish schools were organized. In the year 1364, almost six and a half centuries ago, the Cracow Academy [the University of Cracow] was founded. This was our first institution of higher learning, at a time when Vienna and Leipzig still had no such institutions. Berlin would not have a university for another three hundred years, and Petersburg would not have a university for another four hundred years. By the fifteenth century, the University of Cracow (since 1817 known as the Jagiellonian Univesity) had students coming from all of Europe, even Italy. The university was home to such great minds as the astronomer Mikołaj Kopernik [Nicolaus Copernicus] and the theologian and jurist Paweł Włodkowic [Paulus Vladimiri]. The Cracow Academy's development stalled upon the death of King Kazimierz III Wielki [Casimir the Great], but the institution was re-founded in 1400 by King Władysław II Jagiełło and his wife Saint Jadwiga. In the Founding Act we read: Let there be here the pearl of the powerful sciences, to give to men excellent counsels in maturity, to be a brilliant ornament of the virtues and to be well versed in all skills. May a refreshing fountain of the sciences be opened. Let all draw from its fullness, and let them slake their thirst with the sciences.

We are rightfully proud of the Commission of National Education that was founded in 1773. This was the first ministry of education in Europe. This Commission faced pressure from the movement to secularize education, but it did not surrender. It did not let the heritage of learning from the Church go to waste. This was the same year when the Pope dissolved the Jesuit order which had been dedicated to teaching. In France, when the state assumed control over the schools, they were used to wage war against the Church and tradition, but Poland did not allow the schools to become a tool for indoctrinating the young with ideology. Rather, at a time when Poland was threatened with partition and even after the partition, the schools of the Commission of National Education reinforced the national awareness and cultural identity of Poles. The writer and the deputy Julian Ursyn Niemcewicz also reminded the King: "A free people, o most splendid lord, should be enlightened, otherwise they are not worthy of freedom. In an autocracy where you have no law or rights, but only commands, where the only division is that of master and slave, the rulers base their unlimited power upon ignorance. Then they degrade man's very existence. They confine the range of his awareness. They extinguish the light. They call men only to risk their lives and obey. They do not want anyone to consider things, because if they considered they would no longer obey blindly. A man born on free soil tramples upon such chains. His soul is free of bonds and dares to soar, for he knows his own worth. He knows his nobility. A free man whose destiny may take him anywhere, who can aspire to the highest honors in the land, who can be heard at all levels of government, should become worthy of such honors by education, for the fate of the Fatherland depends upon him. He will be subject only to the law. He should be enlightened, so that he may enact laws that save the people. He should be virtuous, so that he will honor and carry out what he has enacted."[4]

Is not this passage relevant in our time? If democracy is not solidly based upon authentic education, it becomes a concealed form of enslavement. At the same time, people cannot be responsible for public affairs if they have not received a proper academic and moral education, when they have neither competence nor a sense of moral responsibility.

Morality is part of our personal life, and also part of our life in the family and political community. Personal ethics bore fruit among the Poles in some characteristic traits that we may call virtues. We have a high regard for the sense of honor, self-sacrifice, hospitality and good manners. Our great poet, Adam Mickiewicz, wrote of courtesy:

---

4. *Konstytucja 3 Maja 1791* [*The Constitution of May 3, 1791*], Warsaw 1991, IV, pp. 97-98.

Courtesy's not a science too easy, or small.
Not easy, for it is not sufficiently done
With a deftly bent knee, smile at just everyone;
For meseems, such politeness a merchant's is only,
And is not of old Poland, nor yet gentlemanly.
Courtesy's due to all, but not quite in same style,
For not lacking it should be the love of a child,
Or man's public respect to his wife, or a lord's
To his household: with each some distinction accords.
Long must one study, so as to never offend,
And to each the appropriate politeness extend.
And we old, too, have studied: a lord's conversation
Was as the living history of country, of nation,
And, to the gentry, annals of region and shire:
Thus would be made explicit to brother esquire
That he's not an unknown, and is not taken lightly;
So his manners a man would keep under guard tightly.
Today, no one inquires: who are you and where from?
What's your birth, your profession? All as they like come,
If not government's spies, or are not too penurious.
Just as this Vespasianus showed he was not curious
Whence the money, how smelled it, from what hands or place,
They now care not to know a man's manners or race
If he struts and is amply with badges bedecked;
And so friends are respected as Jews gold respect.

(*Pan Tadeusz*, I, 361-385, transl. M. Weyland)

Family life is especially dear to Poles. During the partition of Poland, the life of the nation survived in the family. The family was the nest in which generations of Poles were brought up, where the nation was created by the culture of our forefathers and by a sense of responsibility for the state. One author in the time of the partition wrote: "Some people say that Poland stands because of individuals. It would be more true to say that Poland stands because of the family. [...] The most severe critic in the future will have to recognize that the Polish family carried out its great obligation to be the strongest foundation of citizenship

17

and the nation. It did not abandon its duty even in the worst of times. When everything collapsed into dust, a new life took shape in the family. The Polish family faithfully preserved everything within itself, and this was the condition and guarantee for the rebirth of Poland."[5]

It is a tragedy to see how our home life is dying today. The family has less time together, and the television is an ever-present intruder.

I would like to make a few points about political life. Next to England, Poland is the oldest democratic state. Democracy first developed among the nobility in the fifteenth century, and the Constitution of May 3 (1791) extended democratic rights to the other classes, to the common people and the bourgeoisie. We can read the following in this constitution: "Having thus guaranteed squires all profits due them from the peasants, and desiring as effectively as possible to encourage the multiplication of the people, we declare complete freedom to all persons, both those newly arriving and those who, having removed from the country, now desire to return to their native land, insofar as every person newly arrived from any part, or returning, to the states of the Republic, as soon as he set foot upon Polish soil is completely free to use his industry as and where he will, is free to make agreements for settlement, wages or rents as and to such time as he agrees, is free to settle in city or countryside, and is free to reside in Poland or to return to whichever country he wish, having previously acquitted such obligations as he had freely taken upon himself."[6]

The state ratified by the constitution was home to many nations, and so the constitution was not an expression of nationalism. It was home to Poles, Lithuanians, Belorussians, Russians, Jews, Germans, Latvians, Tartars, Armenians and Gypsies. Several languages enjoyed equal recognition under the law. The union of Poland and Lithuania was unique in its time, and is still an example in this time of ethnic conflicts. It had lasted three

---

5. *Komisja Edukacji Narodowej* [*The Commission of National Education*], Wrocław 1954, p. 426f.
6. W. Łoziński, *Życie polskie w dawnych wiekach* [*Polish Life in the Past Centuries*], Cracow 1958, p. 153.

hundred years and it was only the aggression of the great powers that put an end to it. Today international treaties and organizations are dominated by the language of special interests and politics, but the union of Poland and Lithuania was at a deeper level that reflected a more profound sense of civilization. In the treaty that ratified the Union in the year 1413 we read: "Love does not work in vain. Love radiates within itself. It extinguishes hatred, lessens resentment, unites the divided, raises those who are fallen, levels inequality, sets straight the crooked, supports each and does no harm to any. Whoever takes refuge under the wings of love will be safe and will not fear any harm. Love creates laws and rights, rules kingdoms, lays the foundations of states, and leads the commonwealth to a good condition. He who has contempt for love will lose everything."[7]

In its time of greatness, Poland defended Europe against the onslaught of the Turks. It was considered to be the first line of defense for the civilized world, the outer wall of Christendom. King Władysław III Warneńczyk, barely twenty years old, responded to the request of the emperor of Byzantium John Paleologos. He took arms to defend the emperor against the Turks, and died near Varna in 1444. King Jan III Sobieski saved Vienna in 1684. During the partition and wars, Poles fought on many fronts throughout the world, and their rallying cry was "for our freedom and yours". Kościuszko and Pułaski fought for America's freedom during the American Revolution, and Polish soldiers fought in World War II (e.g. Polish pilots who effectively protected English air during the Battle of Britain). The great Polish theologian and jurist, Paweł Włodkowic, was perhaps the first to voice before the world the special respect and love that Poles have for freedom. In the fifteenth century, he addressed the Council of Constance, proclaiming that every nation had the right to sovereignty, and no one had the right to infringe upon that, even for the loftiest purposes. Even in the name of religion, no one had the right to invade and conquer another state.

---

7. M. Pawlikowski, *Dwa światy* [*Two Worlds*], London 1952, p. 188.

We have already mentioned Polish literature, but Polish art also flourished in architecture, painting, theater and music. The music of Fryderyk Chopin has many national elements, including echoes of folk music and the music of the nobility. It arouses the admiration not only of people in the western world, but Japanese and Chinese find it very expressive. Polish musical forms and rhythms have become part of our universal musical canon. Musicians are familiar with the Polonaise, the Mazurka and the Cracovienne, and of course the various forms of folk music included under the term "Polka". The Polish soul is reflected in Polish art. Ignacy Jan Paderewski said: "None of the other nations in the world can boast of the same wealth of sentiments and moods. The hand of God has played upon the strings of the harp of this nation in tones quiet and plaintive, or powerful and strident. We have the gentleness of love and the valor of great deeds. We have lyricism like a great and swelling wave, and the courage of knights. We have the longing of young girls and manly prudence. We have the tragic sadness of the old and the lighthearted merriment of the young. Perhaps this is the source of our enchanting charm, and perhaps it is also a great shortcoming."[8] Chopin most fully expressed this complex soul in his music. We have such famous painters as Chełmonski, Matejko, Brandt, and the Kossaks, whose works adorn galleries world-wide, including American galleries. Polish art often takes its theme from Poland, its natural life, its people and history.

Christianity has been the dominant religion in Poland, but there have been other religions. There were no religious persecutions in Poland, especially during the Reformation, which led to much bloodshed in Western Europe. Paweł Włodkowic, whom I mentioned earlier, said: *"Fides ex necessitate esse non debet"* – "Faith should not be the result of coercion." Poland was renowned for its tolerance, and so people of many different creeds took refuge from persecution in Poland. In the sixteenth century, King Zygmunt II August was able to say: "I am not king over human consciences." As early as the eleventh century, Jews fled

---

8. I. J. Paderewski, *Myśli o Polsce i Polonii* [*Thoughts About Poland and Polish Communities*], Paris 1992, p. 65.

to Poland from persecution in Germany, and in time the Jewish community in Poland became the largest in the world, with its own laws, customs, religion and schools, including institutions of higher learning. Some even called Poland *paradisus Iudaeorum* – a paradise for the Jews. During the Second World War the German Nazis had special regulations that applied only in Poland, that the punishment for concealing Jews was the execution of the entire family. At least 2 thousand Poles died in this way, or were sent to the concentration camps. 60 to 100 thousands Jews were saved by the Poles. In light of these facts, the widespread opinion today that Poles are anti-Semites is untrue and extremely unjust.

National cultures are a treasure for the societies that grow within the framework of the nations. National cultures can also contain elements that are both extremely beautiful and universal. The culture of one nation can enrich others, because no culture is perfect and absolutely self-sufficient.

When we take pride in our culture, we are not indulging in chauvinism or nationalism. Chauvinism is a hatred for other nations. Love for a certain national culture does not prevent us from admiring other cultures, just as a fascination with the music of Mozart does not hinder us from appreciating the merits of Beethoven and Vivaldi. Nationalism is the deification of a single nation and the exclusion of others. While I enjoy the music of Chopin, I also find comfort in the music of Sibelius. In turn, when someone cannot identify with any national culture, he may find that his psychic and spiritual life disintegrates, and he may easily drown in mass culture. Mass culture does not reach the depths of the human spirit and it does not ennoble the human spirit.

My admiration for Polish culture does not mean that I idealize this culture or my nation. I recognize the shortcomings and weaknesses. However, I do find in my culture certain ideals and models, a certain direction in human life that seem interesting and beautiful.

When we become participants in Polish culture at a deeper level, we may develop more gracefully and become better as human beings. I could summarize what I mean by saying, that by means of culture we may become more and more fully human.

State – Nation – Fatherland

Independence Day (November 11) makes us reflect upon the basic categories conveyed by the name "Poland". Most of us are preoccupied with personal matters, affairs of the day, which is only natural in peacetime. But great anniversaries remind us that it wasn't always so, that there were also times of war and national bondage; that if people living then had thought only about themselves, Poland and Poles would not exist anymore, or would at best be an ethnic relic, surviving merely as an exhibition piece. It must be said that Poland is a priceless treasure. That's why we must honor great anniversaries and pay homage to the defenders of our Fatherland.

But what is Poland? Poland is a state. Poland is our Fatherland. Poland is a nation. These are not synonymous notions. Poland did not exist as a state for 123 years, but the Fatherland and the nation remained. It is perfectly possible for a state to exist and yet lack a nation or a Fatherland. A state has its policies, its legislation and its administration. It may however, be organized in opposition to its people or be indifferent towards them, and then the people gradually lose their sense of national identity. That was the trend in the so-called People's Republic of Poland: as part of the Soviet communist system, which actually aimed at depriving Poles of their national identity, leaving unimpaired only some elements of national folklore, such as dance or song, while suppressing higher Polish aspirations.

When the state does not conserve land, nature or architecture the Fatherland atrophies. How could we keep identifying with the Fatherland if the land is taken over by foreigners, both national and landscape parks destroyed, and Polish architecture – so splendid and fascinating – totally replaced by soulless post-modernism? What would remain for one to miss? Tarmac, tenements and high rise buildings? Modern technology, useful and welcome as it is, is indifferent towards beauty and history, has no sensitivity, no heart for poetry. It doesn't take much for a bulldozer to bury a brook or to tear down a historic wooden house, thus destroying a segment of our cultural landscape. Irretrievably. That is why national inheritance must be protected.

A normal state, built on the foundations of the Latin Civilization, must synchronize the above elements. Only then can its inhabitants feel at home, and only then do they know that it is their state, their land, their culture and their language and these are their compatriots. Our enemies have always tried to disintegrate these elements, and they continue to do this. No wonder that building a sound state is not so simple. It calls for great alertness and stamina. After the fall of communism, the process of healing the contaminated social structure is still ongoing, and here we are told that no one needs independence nowadays, that we must give up sovereignty and Fatherland. This is the strategy devised by... the Euro-socialists. However, it is their problem that they do not know who they are. *We know who we are.*

A modern state can easily degenerate into a bureaucratic monster that devours its own people. No wonder that people distance themselves from such a state. They become withdrawn, do not want to hear anything about the state, and, as a last resort, start looking for a new place on Earth.

This is the basic problem that may plague a state in peacetime. For some individuals political infighting and the struggle for power become an aim in itself. When such individuals come to power they lose all good sense, and they become insane and dangerous, which, in turn, makes people of higher intellectual and moral standards turn away in distaste. They won't enter a political world that has degenerated into a series of tavern brawls, and if they are educated professionals, they won't risk dissipating their talents. This is how the phenomenon of spiritual emigration is born, and it easily turns into actual emigration.

Emigration has become a fundamental problem for our country. It is naïve to appeal to patriotism to stop people from emigrating. Young people are eager to live a full life, they look for prospects, and they want to earn a reasonable wage. When the only prospect at home is vegetation until retirement age, they opt to go abroad. The number of young people leaving our country is staggering. It is a totally new phenomenon, incomprehensible to the older generation that was accustomed to low living standards and poor professional prospects.

On the other hand, people with high qualifications cannot be expected not to leave their homeland if there is no employment adequate to their education at home. Various lobbies, which were once called cliques, usually connected to the former communist party, or secret services, effectively block the academic or professional careers of many talented Poles. So they leave, find employment and recognition abroad, work as professors, engineers, architects, doctors and business people. Only some time later, from a distanced perspective, they realize how careers and good employment were controlled by local mediocrities back home. If this does not change we will keep losing both talented people and our youngsters. In peacetime, professionals cannot be asked to remain in an occupational backwater, neglect their families, and sink into frustration. Times have changed and, in peacetime, work, career and family come first, public matters second. Public duties cannot overshadow one's career and family duties.

Our nation has become scattered all over the world. Poles are practically everywhere. Word has it that in Ireland there are already villages with more Polish than Irish inhabitants. Some emigrants lose their sense of national identity very fast. Dazzled by the new surroundings and by a higher standard of living, they switch to the new language and fail to teach their children Polish. There are others, though, who reinforce their Polishness instead and make sure that their children master immaculate Polish. Much depends on the culture people bring from home and on whether they live amongst their compatriots. It also depends on whether the children are raised in a Polish or a mixed marriage. These are complicated issues.

We, for whom Poland will forever remain the only Fatherland, have to persevere in order to guard that astounding fire of faith, love and hope that has burned for over a thousand years.

These are unfathomable feelings embedded in the depths of our souls. These matters are not easy to talk about. Only a poet like Zygmunt Krasiński could write about them:

Into this immortal fatherland,
Indivisible despite divisions,
Onto this beloved land,
Onto this land – this land of ours,
A tribe of new people shall arrive;
Such as have never been seen before!

(Z. Krasiński, Break-day, Przedświt, 946-951)

How Stalin, Roosevelt and Churchill Decided the Fate of the World

Sometimes it is worth asking simple questions. One such question is where was the Polish People's Republic born. The answer is simple. It was born in the head of one man, the dictator of the Soviet Union, Joseph Stalin. Some acclaimed Polish poets extolled his wisdom (Adam Ważyk) and eulogized his smile (Artur Międzyrzecki), compared him to the sunrise (Stanisław Jerzy Lec) and to a lofty oak (Jan Sztaudynger). He was not only the craftiest of charlatans but also the greatest criminal that mankind has known. The idea of creating an improbable state, named the Polish People's Republic, was born in his head.

The creation of this state was approved by the two Western powers, personally by the President of the United States, Franklin Delano Roosevelt, and the Prime Minister of Great Britain, Winston Churchill. When the Second World War was coming to an end, these two had to make arrangements concerning the new order in Europe and the world and the question of Poland had to be raised.

For us, two conferences were decisive, the Teheran Conference and the Yalta Conference. We know the official history of these meetings, but we know little about how they were seen from the inside. So let's have a look at the memoirs of the American president's son, Elliott Roosevelt, who took part in both, either sitting at the talks or listening to his father's direct accounts.

We are first struck by the fact that during his stay in Teheran the President of the mightiest power of the world did not reside at the American legation, but at... the Soviet one. Yes, President Roosevelt stayed at the Soviet Embassy full of bugs and agents. Stalin, tenderly called "Uncle Joe" by Americans, graciously placed the main building at his disposal, himself moving to some smaller house in the compound (see: Elliott Roosevelt, *As He*

Saw It, New York, 1946, p. 173). Such incredibly good fortune, i.e. to have the President of the United States under complete control in one's own place, seldom comes the way of another country's head of state. Then a few nice gestures were enough for Roosevelt to answer his son's question about how he liked Stalin ("You like him?") because "He gets things done, that man. He really keeps his eye on the ball he's aiming at. So, it's a pleasure working with him." (p. 183). The very first evening, the magnanimous host threw a dinner party for his British and American guests. It was a "Russian style" dinner. What did that mean? A lot of food, and many, many toasts. Elliott Roosevelt was invited too, so his is an eyewitness account. Vodka, different wines and champagne were served, and there was no subject that would not be toasted. At the end, the diners went as far as raising a toast... to the weather. "I wish to propose a toast to the magnificent weather we have been enjoying!" The great statesmen and their entourage happily emptied their glasses. But our observant memoirist noticed that Stalin's glass was refilled from a private bottle. Perhaps he was only drinking water? Ultimately, though, Roosevelt Jr's curiosity was satisfied when, on one occasion, his glass was refilled with the mysterious liquid. It was... one hundred proof. American honor was vindicated, as he writes, for so far he "stuck to the champagne" (p. 187). And such dinner parties were repeated over a period of several days. There were 365 toasts raised, as many as days in a year, until the count was lost on Churchill's birthday ("I am afraid that accurate count was lost.", p. 195). In a word, these three giants, Stalin, Roosevelt and Churchill, while setting the future political order of the world, were utterly drunk. Very likely, though, that Stalin, having the strongest head, even when intoxicated, managed, in all his cunning, to gain the upper hand.

Let's move to Yalta now. Poland was the subject of discussion there as well. Here is how our memoirist relates it: "With respect to Poland, Stalin insisted on the Curzon Line – with minor revisions in favor of the Poles – as that country's eastern boundary, and in the same breath pumped for keeping Poland a strong and self-sufficient nation by adding to its territory in the north and west, at the expense of conquered Germany. A compromise had to be reached in the establishment of a government of Poland which would be in fact a government of national unity: the Russians had a Polish government in Moscow, the British backed the old Polish government operating out of London. Father's [meaning President Roosevelt's] role was mediator and arbitrator – as it was so important for unity that it continue to be" (p. 240).

So it is clear now. Stalin knew exactly what he wanted. That was why he prepared his Polish government in advance. And what difference did it make, anyway, whether it was the Moscow or the London government? Irrespective of the government the country would be strong and self-sufficient. This was the reasoning of these men, and that was what they finally agreed upon. They agreed upon the Moscow government whose founding father was Joseph Stalin, and not the Polish nation. They also agreed on the Curzon Line which, in its initial 1919 version was that of the third partition of Poland, but was constantly being readjusted so that we successively lost the cities of Wilno, Grodno, Tarnopol, and Lvov. Finally, the frontier was set on the River Bug, and all of our Eastern Territories were sliced off.

And this is how the Polish People's Republic was born, totally in the head of Stalin, but with the approval of our allies, Great Britain and the United States, whose representatives couldn't swim in the ocean of liquor as well as Uncle Joe.

This is the history we must be familiar with. We must know it from the inside, as the injustice and suffering of millions of Poles did not come from nowhere. And we experience its consequences to the present day.

Europe Without a Memory?

Although the average man on the street is preoccupied by his daily affairs, looks forward only to the very near future, and ignores the past almost completely, the past still greatly influences both the present and the future, and even the very distant future. It suffices to point out the claims raised by various Septentrions and Hyperboreans, as the writer Henryk Sienkiewicz called peoples and nations whose proper names were protected by censorship in his epoch, and are now protected by political correctness, and who demand huge sums in compensation from Poland. From Poland, that is from those who have been assaulted, robbed, imprisoned, and murdered. We are now called to pay, oftentimes to our oppressors or to cunning profiteers who are rich, cynical, and unyielding. For what reason? Because of the past? But are we speaking of the true past, or a fabricated, manipulated and distorted one? And if it is an untrue, slanted and falsified past, isn't it imperative, isn't it a matter of life and death that we come to know the true past and defend our present and our future?

It is a matter of life and death indeed! We must know the truth about our Polish past, so that we can defend ourselves against recurring attacks and attempts to physically rob us. Anti-Polish propaganda is not a goal in itself, it is the initial stage of a campaign to make us deaf and mute before the actual act of robbery takes place. That's why we must know our history, so that we don't let ourselves be manipulated, don't take the blame for the crimes of others, and aren't victimized, since it is obvious that greed and insolence follow some groups like a shadow, possibly since times immemorial.

However, history also has its much deeper meaning, because it is history that creates what is known as the spirit of the nation. Peoples without history have no spirit. They are like sand in a desert, elusive, shapeless, and characterless. Historical peoples develop their skeleton and muscle in the course of their struggle for survival in order to enjoy the opportunity to pursue their own goals. A people acquire its identity and depth and becomes a nation thanks to its moral attitude, thanks to its scientific and artistic creativity, thanks to its faith. And this means that each member of such a commonwealth can, by identifying with the historical national culture, enrich himself unimaginably, as he embraces the heritage which is the fruit of the endeavors and labors of many generations and the life of millions of human beings.

Teaching history in a self-respecting and conscious nation ought to be the apple of the eye of each school and each family. The Russians knew well what they were doing in the part of Poland under their rule, especially after the fall of the January Rising of 1863, when they brought history teachers from within the Empire to teach Polish history in Russian and from the point of view of Russian interests. No wonder that true history could only be taught in private homes. Many of us also remember how particularly mendacious the history books in the so-called Polish People's Republic (i.e. communist-ruled Poland) were. Symbolic of this phenomenon was the Katyń Massacre whose real perpetrators couldn't be named. But it was not only such outright lies that were dangerous. Even more dangerous was the prospect of perpetuating a falsified picture of Polish history since, according to the guidelines of Marxist ideology, history was supposed to have been one continuous course of class struggle. According to this principle, the Polish nobles were always presented in the worst possible light, and Polish kings stripped of all glamor. A young man didn't have heart to identify with such history, so in most cases he simply rejected it. Thus entire generations grew up not knowing the history of their own nation.

And now we are hearing of new plans. The European Union intends to introduce a history textbook whose use would be obligatory in all member states. Such plans raise a multitude of doubts. One has the impression that this project aims at "smoothing" the history of Europe, so that reference to history would not awaken antagonisms and that all European nations would live in harmony, eventually merging into one European nation. Such a perspective may seem encouraging or even rosy. But it is an absolute pipe dream and a dangerous manipulation as well. There is no such thing as a European nation because Europe is itself made up of many nations. A new nation cannot be established mechanically. It would require time, work and the experience of many generations. If the officials in Brussels nevertheless insist on creating a European nation, they will try to destroy real historical nations, and the means to this end is obliterating their history. This is the purpose which the new textbook of European history will most likely serve. It will be history without history, a mixture of fairy tales and ideology, with all the real conflicts, their true grounds and lasting effects, erased from memory.

What is the lesson to be drawn from all of this? Let's study history, very thoroughly and with comprehension, so that we are aware of the hidden objective of the attempts to deprive us of it, in order that we will not allow ourselves be robbed of identity, whose crucial part is precious historical memory.

A Superpower Still Invisible?

We sometimes wonder who it is in Poland that coordinates the mass media in such a blatantly anti-Catholic and anti-Polish way. There must be some coordination if almost the same second they all focus on one particular subject and then they begin their barrage. Sometimes they will attack a project. Another time a group of people will be bear the brunt and at yet another time a specific person will be at the receiving end of the assault. They will keep shooting day and night, calm down, change the subject, and start all over again. Upon closer inspection, one has the impression that the action had been scripted many days, weeks if not even months in advance. At some moment they push a button in their computers, and out pour virulent texts, filled with aggression, streaked with envy, bloated with fury. Sometimes it seems incredible that anyone could hate Poland and the Church so much. But they can.

On the one hand, they announce to all and sundry that we are free, that Poland is independent; on the other, they watch with the eyes of a hawk for any sound and noble sign of Polish patriotism to nip it in the bud. They soar above Poland like a Sputnik and spy where to swoop down and grab their prey in their talons and drag it all over the world's media, pinning this or that label on it or just hurling insults at it. And then they celebrate victory: Radio Maryja won't get funding for its geothermal project! What good fortune, folks! Watch them rejoice that one more Polish initiative has been thwarted, that Poles won't spread their wings once again. And they go about it in a way duplicitous enough to make Poles rejoice with them, as though their success were a national victory.

What gives one pause is why these anti-Polish actions are not kept in the dark, but rather advertised in such an ostentatious way as though everything were fine, as though the country was saved from a real threat, as though the greatest danger were… Poles themselves. Why do they pursue this in such a conspicuous way? What is the reasoning behind it?

These are actions addressed not to Poles. They are gestures of idolatry addressed to someone else. They arise from the political system that Poles have now, a system in which those who come to power, if they command a working parliamentary majority, are free to do whatever they please. They are beyond the Nation's means of control. They are free to sell all of Poland, to ruin us totally, to send us into bondage. As soon as they capture power and realize its extent, they acquire self-assurance that soon turns into arrogance. The more they have to humble themselves before some foreign power, the more they take revenge on the Polish people. But why does the general public not see this? Because they engineer this thwarting of native initiatives by provoking the envy of man against man, based on the principle: it serves them right! This is possible when the public is being impoverished, as it makes envy spread. People who are getting worse and worse-off initially look if there aren't some others who are better-off than they are, and, once they spot them, they direct all their resentment and anger not at those who hold power and are responsible for the deteriorating conditions, but at those who succeed or those who do not surrender so easily. This is the rationale behind the continuing process of the simultaneous impoverishment and the creation of antagonism in Polish society of today.

In order to understand this, one must grasp the correlation between these two elements. The authorities cannot allow people who understand and deplore the process of our being dispossessed of our material and spiritual inheritance to unite. That's why they constantly look for victims against whom to set some segment of the populace; let some attack and let the others defend themselves. Let one bite the other to death. In the mouths of politicians and newspeople, words like "Pole" or "Poles" start to sound more and more frequently like synonyms of natives who should be measured, weighed, and then sold or silenced. Their emotions are measured, their preferences weighed, they are sold as *Gastarbeiters*, silenced as patriots. The understanding of current events is controlled by the media, the knowledge of the past controlled by the Ministry of Education, while the future, though planned in advance, must remain veiled, must surprise, raise hopes and provoke fear and even dread. The masses must not be indulged. They are supposed to work, pay taxes, sleep, and be afraid. They must be kept in a constant state of fear, shown as many misfortunes as possible, including accidents and crimes imported from the farthest corners of the globe.

Murderers and perverts are popular heroes nowadays. They are presented, talked about, written about, exploited to the limit by the media. They are there to frighten and to poison the general atmosphere. Fear paralyzes, deprives of the clarity of thought, it is essential in order that people don't see and grasp the general design. But what is this design?

It had been drafted much earlier than officially claimed when postwar Christian Democrats like Adenauer or Schuman are recalled. Let's not be naïve. One of our eminent historians presented a short but fascinating and prophetic text in which we read: "From the League [of Nations] a superstate will grow, a supranational state with executive, legislative and judiciary branches, with penal codes, civil and procedural. There will be direct elections to its parliament, an International Bank, a unified currency [...] which will make it easier for individual states to pay up their debts...". Has this not been largely implemented already? And the author, Władysław Konopczyński, wrote it in 1925 in an essay entitled "The Invisible Superpower", published in the magazine *Przegląd Wszechpolski* [*All-Polish Review*]. This 'Superpower' is being built according to an almost hundred-year-old plan, which has little in common with Christianity, and what is more, as we read, the powers behind it aim at equality, fraternity and liberty, destroying the foundations of the existing social system in their way, dismembering and crushing nation-states, and enslaving individuals in fetters of pitiless collectivism. These plans vary in details, but one emotion unites them by an inextricable tie: their inhumane hatred of religion. It is in this that the essence of the design is hidden, and not in the pious but naïve plans of the so-called Founding Fathers of the EU. A design differing from their plans is being implemented today, the design of a superpower which Konopczyński called "the invisible superpower".

34

On the Need for Local Elites

The domination of the media in public life results, among other things, in the lack of elites in local communities. Only megastars promoted by television, radio or the press count. But stars endorsed by the media are not necessarily genuinely worthy. They are often purely virtual entities, inhabiting only the space of electronic communications. However, it is real people, the actual inhabitants of a neighborhood or village, who ought to make a genuine local community. Without the backing of such a community, loneliness, which cannot be assuaged by any TV program, creeps into our lives. We watch television alone, listen to the radio alone and read the paper alone. A human being naturally desires to be part of a community for a number of reasons, beginning with the natural instinct drawing us towards others, and ending with participation in great projects, which cannot be carried out by just one individual alone.

The social dimensions of work are not a solution to the craving for life in a community. Although we generally work with other people, work as such aims at some definite goal set within the framework of a business. Some will manufacture bottle caps, others furniture, still others engines. However, human beings need broader human contacts which gratify their cultural needs on the one hand and on the other, include them in the life of a social unit within an administrative structure.

When visiting various communities in Poland, one gets the impression of prevailing discouragement and apathy. At first, it seems to come from the difficult material situation, or perhaps from some family problems. But sooner or later, the right approach changes the mood, people become more lively, more eager, and even manage to laugh. But why? The fact is that direct contact, mingling with others, discovering the right perspective, welcoming the gift of wisdom, kindness and humor, is something people are in desperate need of in order to function normally, perceive what is good and fight what is evil. It's so simple and banal, and yet so often forgotten nowadays.

Naturally, there must be someone who will set the right tone for these get-togethers; a person offering something of value, having some prestige. Since there are not that many megastars, it is essential that some local stars, appreciated for their talents or their ethos, are available. When looking back at the interwar years, listening to reminiscences or reading memoirs, we see that numerous local events attended by local celebrities were organized in local communities, so that people could meet and mingle, enjoy one another's company, or just see others. Occasions varied. It could be a parade after a marksmen's competition, a speaking contest or a brassband concert. Nowadays, if anything happens it is either political, e.g. a pre-election meeting, or has a business angle, e.g. a fair, while there are no events having a purely social character.

Warsaw is divided into districts. Each district is headed by a mayor, who has his deputies and his staff; there are also district councillors. There is also a district police chief who has his personnel. There is a fire department. Different local offices and organizations could be named and listed. But how many of us, inhabitants of a city district or town, have ever actually seen the people running them? Hardly anybody. Everything is so impersonal, nameless, indeed depressing.

Not all of this can be blamed on economic hardships, on poverty or illness. When the Holy Father visited Poland, people were moved by a new spirit, they were together, bound by something noble, and drawn to Him. They aren't any poorer today, but somehow they are sad. The cause is simple: public life lacks spirit. This spirit does not come from nowhere. Basic social ties that bind local communities must be restored.

Indeed, the only place where we meet at least once a week is church. We know the parish priest, we know his curates, and we feel appreciated by them. Were it not for the church, we would hardly have a place to meet at all. It is the Church that preserves the old, Roman (and even pre-Christian, which does not necessarily mean bad), ways of organizing social life.

36

The present-day public administration has no idea how to go about this. Civil servants just keep their office hours and sit in their offices. In fact, it is fortunate if they sit there at all and commendable if they do some honest work, but social life calls for something more. A void has been created here. It would pay to reactivate time-honored Polish traditions that help integrate local communities. These are the real, not virtual settings of our life. It is a challenge facing the mayors of our towns and city districts as well as by village elders. They would certainly earn the gratitude of their citizens.

The Discretionary State?

In recent years, we often hear the term "law-governed state" repeated with particular relish by communists and liberals. It is usually quoted as opposed to the religious state ruled by clerics and governed by the principles of religion. But looking more closely at the actual functioning of the Polish state we see that in numerous situations it is not a law-governed and even less a religious state, but rather a discretionary state. This means that what is practiced is what some people, at their discretion, decide is right. Are such decisions against the law? Not at all! They are in accordance with the letter of the law. But what really is this "law"? The law today is a set of regulations enacted by various statutes, and recorded in the "Law Gazette" or the Penal Code. But the situation is not that simple. If it were there would be no need for judges, prosecutors, or lawyers. We have all three in abundance.

So matters must be complicated. But why are they complicated? Legal acts use specialized vocabulary, just like science, a vocabulary that not everyone can comprehend. In order to master it, one has to pursue special studies that all aspiring jurists must complete. However, even though they are licensed jurists, they argue with one another and they have been arguing forever. Why? Because the law must not only be understood but also interpreted. The decision must be made in accordance with the particular article of the code by which a case is to be heard. Then, at each stage of every case, jurists may have differing opinions. So the matter will go from one court to the next, sometimes ending up as high as the level of the Constitutional Tribunal. Then, when all is settled, final doubts often remain.

Such was the case of the validity of the mandate of the Mayor of Warsaw. Some people thought that the judgment was tainted by the judges' politics, i.e. that it was biased. Others rejoiced that the will of the electorate prevailed. For an average person, it is difficult to decide. Previously, under communism, the situation seemed simpler. Apart from the clearly political trials, what counted was the amount of the bribe. What is the situation today?

It must be pointed out that in the face of such controversies, invoking the rule of a "law-governed state" is simply pulling the wool over people's eyes. Law as a set of regulations doesn't mean anything. If it did, a good computer program would be sufficient. A question would be entered and, within seconds, the answer would appear. A law-governed state is, in fact, a state of people who must comprehend and interpret the law, and on its basis decide whether this or that act was in accordance with the law or not. The human factor is predominant here. The jurists must be interpreting a specific law in the way they wish if their opinions differ diametrically or, indeed, contradict each other. Further, if it is up to them to decide, the higher someone is placed, the greater weight his say carries. When we turn to the highest offices of the land, i.e. the cabinet ministers, parliamentary leaders, the President, even though they are representatives of the state, they do whatever they think is right at their discretion. Thus, the settings and decorations may change but there is a human factor behind every decision, from the desk of a village leader to the Presidential Palace. Everywhere there are merely human beings, and it is they who decide. Thus although their decisions are supported by the majesty of their offices, these are only external attributes. Neither a village leader's pen, nor a judge's robe, or the President's insignia make the decision. It is always made by a person. Not by the office, but by a person. Not by a commission, but by the members of a commission, i.e. by people. This is the source of a basic misunderstanding, because the final ruling is issued as the decision of a commission, or ministry. It has its legal stamp, so it is not supposed to be the private opinion of one person, even though in fact it is the opinion of an individual acting within the limits of his or her intellectual capacity, moral sensitivity and position in a certain group.

Spaniards, when commenting the *modus operandi* of this or that commission, refer to the prevalence of what they call *amigos* and *bandas*. *Amigos* translate to "friends" and *bandas* to "buddies", and more bluntly, "cliques". Buddies have their buddies, but also their enemies, and cliques may be connected to other cliques, and at variance with other ones still. When passing a sentence or taking a position in a case, *amigos y bandas* have to perform some cagey maneuvering not to commit a blunder. It would be a pity to lose one's membership in a commission that brings one numerous friends.

The conclusion in this case is very simple. One must watch out for appearances and examine people carefully. An office does not enhance one's brain power. It simply broadens the range of one's responsibilities and possibilities. That is why the way public personalities are created and their individual culture and moral integrity are so essential. In a situation when the most important decisions have discretionary character, what is vital is who makes the decision and not what robe he or she wears, or what office he or she occupies. What matters is whether such a person looks out for *amigos* and *bandas*, or works for the benefits of the citizens and communities for whom he, or she is responsible.

Democracy equals a discretionary state. If people without vision and ethos gain power, they will keep talking about a law-governed state merely to hide their own ignominious deeds. Whereas if we succeed in raising a generation of morally and intellectually sound people, there is a big chance that even democracy will not bring us harm.

Knocking Out the Catholic Church

A merciless campaign to eliminate the Roman Catholic Church from public life began with the French Revolution. It was aimed not only at its political influence, although this was naturally of primary importance, but also at morality, art, learning, and schools, or more or less, at civilization. This process is still continuing. Different methods were used, both brutal and subtle. French and Bolshevik revolutionaries did not hesitate to resort to the most brutal of measures. They imprisoned, shot, hanged, and drowned people of the Church. Churches and other church-related buildings were devastated, destroyed, and blown up, or, at best, were converted into museums, warehouses or stables. Different methods were employed in different countries, and the resistance patterns differed as well. Some people surrendered right away, others went underground, still others resisted until the very end. The biggest problem was carrying a living faith over to new generations who were subjected form the youngest years, since preschool in fact and in most cases compulsorily, to the process of brainwashing but especially to anti-religious indoctrination.

Vast expanses of Europe have been totally secularized, and are blank areas today. Churches there are practically deserted, and schools, including institutions of higher learning, even though they may still bear the traditional Catholic names, have very little if nothing in common with Catholicism. Such is the situation for instance, in Belgium. Some other countries that were predominantly religious until recent times, have revealed greater and greater cracks during the last dozen years or so. In Spain, the Socialists who have come to power keep passing, as though out of spite, the most outrageous laws aimed at the foundations of Christian morality. In Ireland, only five priests were ordained last year. Now, Poland's turn has come.

Some recent events shook our public opinion. Polish-language papers, uncannily synchronized, took on the air of worried custodians of morality, law and order by raising an outcry against former agents of the communist secret police and such Judases in the Church. These were the same papers that had for years been systematically combating the Church, or at least striking at the very foundations of the Polish Christian heritage.

Present methods of fighting the Church are not particularly sophisticated. Their effectiveness rests on the short memory of the mass audience of the mass media, and on dulling people's brains through shock. The news that a priest has stolen a million dollars is shocking. Then while public opinion remains in shock, fueled day after day by new cunningly dispensed details, the process of lowering the prestige of the Church proceeds, gradually reducing its influence on public life. The point being promoted is that a priest's voice should count for nothing, that the faithful should see a thief in every man of the cloth.

In Ireland and the United States, accusations of pedophilia turned out to be a very effective method of fighting the Church. Trials not only lower the social prestige of the Church, they also expose it to costs running into millions of dollars. Each accusation brought to court is in a flash taken up and spread by the most powerful media as news of the highest importance. Afterwards, no one follows up whether the accusation was actually true or not. The point is that an accusation was made. The mass audience is not interested in such "marginal" details as whether the accused party was indeed guilty or not. When the verdict finally turns out to be not guilty, the media will most likely not correct the false accusation, or if they do, they'll do it as inconspicuously as possible. Meanwhile, they will hold their breath watching for the next affair in the Church, with teeth bared and ready to snap.

What about Poland? Since the time "communism" was installed in Poland, we had enough examples. In the Stalinist years, accusations of collaboration with imperialist powers were common. Communists accused priests, even bishops of being spies. Show trials were advertised nationally (see the case of Bishop Czesław Kaczmarek of Kielce). Sentences were cruel, and the suffering unimaginable. Bugs were planted in the diocesan curias, young agents were sent to infiltrate seminaries, and priests were intimidated and blackmailed. The assault on the Church was institutionally organized and run by ministries and state agencies. However, in spite of all this, in spite of human frailties, the Church prevailed.

Then "freedom" and "independence" came. Former communist bosses and their heirs ingratiated themselves with John Paul II, participated in masses and pilgrimages, posed for photos and films. They were beside themselves with esteem and admiration. But at the same time, secret services kept working and preparing themselves for different scenarios and developments.

During recent years, the "Irish scenario", i.e. accusations of pedophilia, was attempted several times. Accusations without any proof and based on trumped up testimony were levied, and priests were robbed of their good names and disgraced. Some were even removed from their offices. That is how strong the "former" communists still are! Nevertheless, their actions backfired. In the end, the common sense of the faithful prevailed. So the detractors reverted to the "Stalinist scenario", though in a roundabout manner. Formerly, the "communists" accused clerics of collaboration with the West, now they accuse them of collaboration with... themselves, i.e. with "communism." Then as during the communist era, before anything is proven, an uproar is created all over the world. Maybe the public prestige of the Church will finally fall, they reason. Maybe the recipe of the Nazi propagandist, Dr. Joseph Goebbels (whose idea this was), will work and the Church will "lock itself in the vestry."

Accusations of theft, sexual activities, pedophilia and spying are time-tested methods aiming to knock out the Church in Poland. None of us is in the position to pass judgment, but we must know what purpose such showy actions serve. They are not for the sake of truth or justice, and certainly not out of concern for the Church. Thus we must maintain common sense and not abandon the Church, which has not failed us so far. We must certainly not abandon it to be judged by these untrustworthy "moralists."

The Price of Emigration

More and more Poles go abroad to earn a living nowadays. In most cases it is not illegal work anymore. Presently, a welder may work on an official contract in most member-states of the European Union, and though he barely knows the language, he can earn three times as much as a university professor in Poland who happens to know ten languages. No wonder then that learning fares worse and worse in Poland, while shipbuilding and construction of industrial complexes fares better and better in some other countries. Students don't go on vacation any more, don't rest in the mountains, on the lakes or in the woods after a year of hard studying, but spend summer months working in a foreign pub or on a construction site. Many of them will not come back home, and if they do they will be thinking about the next trip since the saved money won't last long. Studies at institutions of higher learning have taken on a mass character, while losing the atmosphere of personal contacts and friendships of a community engaged in the search for the truth. Everyone is absorbed by the search for employment now. The academic atmosphere is changing. Something is coming to an end. There are no prospects for graduate students since postgraduate studies are very expensive and becoming even more so. And what's the use of earning a PhD anyway? Consequently there are few candidates, and even those who begin, often get discouraged and give up midway.

In a few or a few dozen years, our country will be changed beyond recognition. A sudden collapse will come, and we will become something else. The law of generation change will take its toll. There will be no possibility of return for many an emigrant, no possibility or return to the home country or the family.

What kind of family are we speaking of anyway if one of the spouses works permanently in another country? Means of support are indispensable, but the lack of an actual parental presence at home cannot be replaced by a telephone conversation, a toy or a fancy piece of clothing brought home once a year. Members of a family who do not physically live together on a daily basis lose touch with each other, stop interacting and influencing each other and turn into strangers. The longing accumulated during the absence is replaced by a short-lived joy upon return, but soon the togetherness becomes tiring. For growing children, the physical absence of a mother or father is an irreparable loss. It cannot be made up for by a short vacation, or twenty years later, after retirement, when the adult children have gone their separate ways.

So perhaps the entire family going abroad is a better prospect? A lot depends on the mentality and personal culture of the individuals involved. If a person is strong and looks at life from the perspective of acquiring possessions, he or she may be happy abroad. For how long? The greatest drama of emigrants is their children losing their national identity. Let us entertain no illusions about this. Children quickly melt into the community of their peers, and since their peers will be kids of a different nationality, even though they have Polish roots themselves, their national identity, manifesting itself in their language, mentality, way of life, and the hierarchy of values, will take on a different character. Thus, parents who decide to emigrate must in advance accept that their children will not be Poles. At the most, in the interim period, they will become nationless individuals, torn between the country of their parents' origin and the country of settlement. Why should a John or an Elizabeth born far from Poland be inspired by our history, our monuments and our landscape? These will be meaningless for them. They will be somebody else's memories, a world of their parents' past and their impotent nostalgia. National identity is formed by the country's nature, culture, language, and the community in which one lives. Children of emigrants, cut off from all of this, will not be Poles even if their ancestors had been Poles for twenty generations.

Their being cut out from that chain of Polish generations is a loss not only for Poland, but equally for themselves. It is a great deprivation. Belonging to the Polish nation means being part of a continuum of definite historical events and ideals, being elevated onto a higher plane, having a new spirit added to life. Our presence in European and even world history had and continues to have its moral and religious dimensions. We must remain spokesmen for the opposition to the loss of soul by the West. In this lies the sense of remaining part of our nation. It should be treated not as a manifestation of megalomania, but as a challenge, even a sacrifice if need be.

As a free man, opting for emigration, I would not ask how much I would earn, but whether I wanted to belong to another nation and, as a consequence, to its past to and to its present. The response to such a question would definitely be an emphatic "no", even if I were to be paid a hundred times more. I would not want to belong to the nation of Goethe, or Shakespeare, or Molière. I prefer to belong to the nation of Jan Kochanowski and Juliusz Słowacki, of Krzysztof Kamil Baczyński and Zbigniew Herbert. It is them that I understand; no other great men are as close to my heart. I could not fathom removing them from the generations of my descendants. My conscience would not allow it.

Origins of the USSR

Though it may strike us as a truism, it must be reiterated that the Polish People's Republic cannot be comprehended without a reference to the Soviet Union. Over a quarter of a century after the infamous revolution, our country wound up as an outer region of the empire that over the years kept enlarging the territory "inherited" from Tsarist Russia. Poland was to be a Soviet republic on a microscale.

These origins are most important in the rich history of the Soviet Union because it was then that the basic principles of communist civilization were crystallized. The literature of the subject is overabundant, but there is one especially interesting book, the 1924 *Impressions from Soviet Russia* by Charles Sarolea. Sarolea, a Belgian who taught French literature at the University of Edinburgh. He was very friendly towards Poles and penned a charming little book, *Letters on Polish Affairs* (1922). He was an astute observer and an excellent writer. He did not favor his left eye nor did he turn his eyes away. Perhaps that's why his name and his writings are so little known today. Thus, all the more reason to find out what Sarolea saw in the Soviet Union a few years after the revolution. What he observed will still frighten or amuse us today. Let us see what is a thing of the past and what is still relevant.

The fate of professors in the new land of the Soviets was significant. Those who survived and did not escape abroad, even if they kept their university positions, earned so little that they had to seek additional income either by selling the saved remnants of their possessions, or, "by doing odd jobs for the Government" (p. 12). Even so, they could be fired any day. How many left? Hundreds. In Berlin alone there were so many that a Russian university was established, and Czechoslovakia filled around 300 (!) university chairs with Russian professors (p. 25). Further, how many were murdered? Thousands. Sarolea assesses their number at nine thousand. That's how many professors were killed by the communists. It shows that the murder of Polish professors during World War II by either the Soviets or the Germans amounted to only a microscale of what had been going on in the Soviet Union at the bloody onset of the creation of a new society.

Do you remember the phrase "dictatorship of the proletariat"? Here is what the Belgian author writes about it: "In order to disguise the brutal facts Lenin called his new tyranny by the high-sounding name 'Dictatorship of the Proletariat'". But the words 'Dictatorship of the Proletariat' are an empty phrase and a contradiction in terms. "Especially in view of the fact that 90% of Russian society was illiterate at the time, and so a blend of two words of Latin origin was mere sounds without any real meaning to them". It carried some meaning, though. "The regime established in November 1917 is not a Dictatorship of the Proletariat, but a Dictatorship over the Proletariat, and the dictators themselves are neither proletarians nor workers. In almost every case they are intellectuals, they either belong to the higher nobility, like Cicerin, or to the small landowner class, like Lenin, or to the Jewish middle-class, like Trotski-Bronstein, or Zinoviev-Apfelbaum, or Radek-Sobelson. In nine cases out of ten they are writers and journalists" (p. 40).

Thus at the head of the Soviet State were people about whom anything could be said but that they were peasants or workers; and few of them were indigenous Russians. They called their tyranny a dictatorship, but since it was not the dictatorship of the proletariat, it was dictatorship, despotism, tyranny over the proletariat, as Sarolea rightly indicates. This kind of dictatorship over the proletariat prevailed throughout the entire Soviet regime, including the Polish People's Republic, until the very last day of the regime's existence.

Soon Poland will celebrate the ninetieth anniversary of what we call the "Miracle on the Vistula," i.e. the 1920 victory of the Polish forces over the much more numerous invading Soviet army. But why was the Soviet army so numerous? The organizer of the Red Army was Lev Trotsky, but who were the "inductees"? Were they young men flocking to the ranks for patriotic or perhaps ideological reasons? Nothing of the kind. On the one hand, he had unlimited "man power" inherited from the tsarist armies; on the other, "hunger was the best recruiting sergeant for Trotsky." [...] "In the terrible conditions of starvation which began to prevail from the end of 1917, the simplest way to escape the starvation was to join the Red Army" (p. 43). It was these hordes of starving soldiers, in addition mixed up by Trotski as to national origin (Latvians, Armenians, Jews, Georgians, Tartars), that invaded Poland in the first stage of an operation planned to conquer all of Europe. In the next stage, they would join forces with the German communists and socialists. However the Soviets remembered the bitter lesson of their 1920 defeat well, and they waited nineteen years to take their revenge; first on the "Polish lords," and then on all Poles.

Once sometimes wonders what the point of it all was. They murdered others, but they murdered their own as well; those at the top and at the bottom. What was their guiding principle, since, by any sound standards, it seems simply absurd? They waved a few banners, they threw a few slogans, and then the slaughter began, turning the world into a huge slaughterhouse. Whence this demented ideology, whence this blindness? What is even worse, their criminal acts have never been really condemned.

The Illegal Polish People's Republic

For many people, the Polish People's Republic is not only a historical, but also a legal fact. There was a state by this name, it had a legal status, it had its emblem (an eagle stripped of its crown) and its authorities (with legislative, executive and judiciary branches), and it was recognized internationally. And for those born during the years of its existence, it was the one and only Poland, as they knew no other Poland. It was the country of their childhood and their youth, of their professional career, in other words, the land of spring and summer of their lives, always remembered with special fondness. Having its legitimacy called into question may feel for them like being deprived of a part of their life.

However, when we view our history dispassionately from a reasonable distance, it becomes plain that the Polish People's Republic was an illegal state. Yes! And this truth must be brought home to Poles born after the transformation of 1989. They must have their picture of Poland revised, so that they see the importance of defending our statehood, so that they do not leave their native land so lightheartedly as though they were fleeing a People's Republic.

In an excellent article titled "The Elections of 1947: the Founding Myth of Communism" (*Bulletin of the Institute of National Remembrance*, January-February 2007, pp. 106-115), Dr. Maciej Korkuć points out: "After 1939 the legal structures of the Government of the Polish Republic functioned both in Poland and in exile. In the light of both international and Polish law, the fact of the continued existence of the Polish state during the Second World War is incontestable, and this holds true for both the Soviet and German occupations" (p. 106).

Poland had at its disposal all of the components which legal authorities consist of, including the President and the Government, whereas both occupations were totally illegal and unlawful as authorities imposed by the invaders. This includes the so-called

PKWN, or Polish Committee of National Liberation, established toward the end of the war in Moscow by the fiat of the ruler of a foreign state. This ruler resorted to the method recommended by Niccolò Machiavelli that in order to subjugate a country one must appoint a puppet government for it (*The Prince*, Book V). But since when is the ruler of a foreign state empowered to delegalize the legally operating authorities of another state, and appoint a new government instead? It sounds absurd and tragicomic, as does the accompanying explanation that PKWN is "the governing body of the sovereign Polish State." A sovereign governing body indeed: it was established in Moscow, had no connection whatsoever to the Polish authorities legally operating since 1939, and had nothing in common with the will of the Polish nation. By whose ruling should it be a government and be sovereign? But PKWN – the "pride" of communists – is just a "body" on which the legitimacy of Polish People's Republic was based.

When the war was over, however, communists needed some "legitimization," so that they could pretend to meet democratic standards and claim before the world: we are in power here because that is what the nation wants. The West would recognize the Polish People's Republic only under the condition that a free election be held. To tackle this challenge, the communists launched a large-scale operation according to a precisely devised scenario. Terror on the one hand, i.e. the imprisonment and murder of ideological opponents, and on the other, political pushing and shoving, and a huge propaganda campaign at home and abroad.

Nevertheless, their chances of actually winning the election were infinitesimal. What would be their solution? A referendum as a test. However, friendly help was needed in order to probe the ways of securing the required results. Dr. Korkuć writes: "The falsification of the referendum results was supervised by a group of specialists in preparing and doctoring documents, sent to Warsaw by Stalin on June 20, 1946, and commanded by Col. Aaron Palkin, head of Department D of the MGB (Ministry of National Security) of the USSR. On June 22, Palkin and the chief (Soviet) advisor to the (Polish) Ministry of National Security, Col. Semyon Davidov, discussed the technical details of the operation with (Władysław) Gomułka (General Secretary of the ruling Polish Workers' Party) and (Bolesław) Bierut (the acting Polish president by Soviet appointment). In the course of the falsification operation, MGB officers prepared 5,994 reports of electoral district commissions, with tallied votes, and forged 40 thousand signatures of commission members" (p. 111). Friendly help indeed, wasn't it? So, in spite of the fact that three quarters of the voters were against, the official report read: 68% in favor.

After such a success, a parliamentary election could be called. On January 10, 1947, Bierut summoned Col. Palkin's team once more. As Dr. Korkuć testifies, "falsification took place in electoral commissions of all levels." Falsification techniques were manifold. In the first place, 3,500 out of 5,500 commissions were manned solely by Polish Workers' Party members who were equipped with spare report sheets and could freely doctor the results. Ballot boxes were changed, candidates of the opposition PSL (or Polish Peasant Party) disqualified, almost half a million voters stripped of their voting rights, and members of the electoral commissions blackmailed into becoming informers of the secret police, the UB [Office of Security] (p. 113).

This is how the communists in power helped the nation "legalize" them. But what if one wants to know the truth? The truth is, as we read, that "the sole source of power for the successive communist governments was the will of the Soviet dictator, Joseph Stalin, and his dictums of the forties and the fifties" (p. 114).

Today we must ask the dramatic question: have we really rid ourselves of that Polish People's Republic of old? How could we if no vetting and decommunization procedures were implemented? How could we if the same people and groups, with their informal connections and secret lobbies, remain untouched? How could we have if so many members of PZPR, the former communist party, and the former communist secret services continue to occupy high positions in state administration, in the media and the education system? One must be aware of this to understand and counteract accordingly, to consciously take part in elections of all kinds (especially when not falsified), and not leave the country of one's birth now when it is in so much need of redemption.

The End of Democracy?

Democracy is one of the vaguest notions, and as a political system, it is the most susceptible to manipulation. Perhaps that is why it attracts so many dishonest, unscrupulous, badly educated and self-interested people. It is a word of Greek origin, so with our present low level of education, its real meaning is hardly comprehended by most people using it. Hence it is variously interpreted, so much so that the system known as democracy took on different historical forms.

The most common definition describes it as government (*kratéo*) by the people (*demos*). The problem is that it is not exactly clear who "the people" are. In ancient Greece, it certainly wasn't what we would presently call "the people": let's say the urban proletariat and the inhabitants of the countryside. The "people" were exclusively free Athenians born of legally married parents who were also free. Neither slaves, nor *métoikos*, or foreign arrivals, were considered "people"; nor were women. Thus the notion of the "Greek people" had a very restricted meaning, and did not correspond to the present-day understanding of democracy. Athenian democracy was strictly limited to free male Athenians.

Since ancient times, wherever a democracy emerges, it must be specified what kind and whose democracy it is, and who are "the people," or the real sovereign of public life? Who can elect the government and who can be elected to serve in the government?

In modern times, absolutism, also known by the Greek terms of "tyranny" or "despotism," prevailed in Europe. England and Poland were two exceptions, with a kind of democracy. Since they were not the democracy of a city-state, but of an entire country, the notion of "the people" was changed as well. The people were... the nobles. Peasants and burghers had no political rights, even though in Poland rights were not limited to Polish nobility, as the nobles of foreign extraction shared the same privileges. It was a relatively large class, consisting of up to 20% of the total population, a phenomenon unparalleled in all of Europe. Thus modern Polish democracy was a democracy of the nobles.

Since the nineteenth century, the division into traditional classes grew more and more anachronistic. States composed of citizens were being established, obliterating the significance of class origin. But is this now already some kind of "unadulterated" democracy? By no means, since democracy is defined not only by who has voting rights, but also by who has the right to be elected and govern. Although the right to vote has become universal, the right to be elected remains significantly limited. It is the parties that have become the real sovereigns of political life. Every citizen of a given state may vote when he or she turns eighteen, but those elected can be only those whose candidacy was entered by one of the parties. One cannot run for the Sejm (Polish parliament) on one's own, and what is more, someone who might obtain the greatest number of votes in the entire country, would not be elected if the party that entered him did not meet the arbitrary threshold of a certain percentage of the total vote.

Present-day democracy is therefore a party democracy. There is one more essential point that must be made. Some voters and not only in Poland, think that they are actually electing their parliamentary representatives. However, nothing could be more erroneous. In ancient Greece, that was how it was. The practice there was that if the elected candidate didn't carry out the voters' program and didn't live up to his promises, he could be removed midterm. This was logical, as he was supposed to represent his electorate.

Nowadays, the constitution allows a deputy to feel free of any responsibility toward his constituents, since the people who voted for him cannot call him to account. That is why politicians say one thing before election and something completely different afterwards; they are totally unaccountable.

The Swiss peasant democracy is an interesting phenomenon in the history of democracy. Established on principles elaborated by Jean-Jacques Rousseau, it is based on referendums on important public questions. They have their significance, reassuring people in their right to decide matters by vote and confirming them as the real sovereign in political life of the country.

But what about Poland? Only God knows. A comparable decline in political manners has never been witnessed. Everything is disguised by the sacrosanct word "democracy." Forty biblical years won't be enough to put the situation back to normal. Half as many have already passed since the transformation of 1989 and there is no improvement is in sight. There is only brutal infighting for party interests, consisting of lies, boorish behavior, manipulation, nepotism. Is this what one calls "Democracy"? No one in their right mind would believe that.

The manipulation and abuses to which present-day democracy is apt to resort are best exemplified by the European Union's campaign to have the so-called Reform Treaty signed by member-states. It is well known that the treaty drastically changes the status of member states, removing them further and further from both sovereignty and the legacy of genuine European culture, which includes Christianity. The way the treaty is being pushed through and axiology it is based on have nothing to do with a democracy erected on the foundations of Western civilization.

It must be clearly spelled-out that the decision to sign, or not to sign, the treaty, which is made solely by politicians, to the exclusion of all other citizens, i.e. without a national referendum, bodes the demise of an already ailing democracy. The treaty is sheer violence, smacking of Byzantium, not of Athens. The Polish government must not and should not sign the treaty without first consulting the nation.

The High Priests of Democracy

P resent-day democracy is a highly complicated political system, reminiscent less and less of what ancient Greeks meant by it. Volumes can be written about the differences between the old and the new democracy, pointing out that the latter is neither government by the people, nor government by the citizens of a given state, but government by a party. Parties often pursue their own interests, or the interests of those who put them in power, or their sponsors. In the last case, democracy morphs into oligarchy, or government by the very rich. Sometimes democracy is also a cover for anarchy as influential socialists promote civil disobedience when some legislation does not suit them, or exposes their strange connections and dependences. So democracy must be watched very carefully nowadays.

Poland has an institution seldom discussed, and if so, only on important occasions. It is called the Constitutional Tribunal. Its role, as defined by the Constitution, is limited to four fields among which the most conspicuous is the constitutionality of enacted laws. The Tribunal adjudicates diverse questions, though some time ago it gagged the Parliamentary Commission for Investigating the Banks, pronounced valid the contested mandate of the Mayor of Warsaw, and thwarted the vetting of people in positions of public trust for suspected past collaboration with the former communist secret police.

What is the general idea of establishing one more institution with such vast powers, an independent constitutional body of the state? It stems from the specifics of the model of democracy adopted in Poland. But not only in Poland. It based on the concept of law structured according to what in modern philosophy is known as the mathematical model. It is worth explaining that in modern times. In the course of the so-called scientific revolution, the fascination with mathematics reached such heights that only what could be converted into the language of mathematics, or at least was structured in the likeness of a theorem, was considered scientifically sound. Even ethics, *more geometrico*, explained by means of geometry, was proposed by the famous seventeen-century philosopher, Baruch Spinoza. This called for axioms from which conclusions could be deduced. The value of a thesis or opinion was measured by its conformity with the axioms. Such a model was adapted for political systems. It is a collection of such axiomatic norms from which the Constitution is made. All laws enacted by parliament must conform to it.

However, law is not geometry and regulations are not numbers that can be easily, almost automatically, fed into a computational system. Law consists of words and sentences that must be interpreted. But when we read in the Constitution that man has the right to live, we may ask who is man and what is life. One person will say that life begins at conception, another that it begins at birth. Thus, obvious matters become complicated, and complicated matters are pronounced to be in conformity with the law. Who says so? The judges, of course, for it is their mandate to interpret the law.

We must not overlook the threat inherent in this. The judges may interpret the law according to who they are, what their general culture is, and how, when and where they were educated. In addition, we cannot forget that in Poland many judges were formed by communist law schools, had communist professors, and were steeped in leftist ideology. This should not be construed as the call for a witch hunt, but an attempt at awakening awareness of the need to watch some institutions from a critical distance, irrespective of their pretty and noble names.

This critical distance is all the more important because some foreign examples are not edifying, either. In the United States, a role similar to that of our Constitutional Tribunal is performed by the Supreme Court. The judges are proposed by the President (in Poland by a group of deputies or the Presidium of the Sejm), and they are confirmed by the Senate (by the Sejm in Poland), with the difference that in Poland they are elected for a nine-year term, and in the States for life.

How did this happen in the United States? When Franklin Delano Roosevelt was elected President, he had the bright idea of filling the Supreme Court with as many people of the left as possible. In consequence, since the sixties, the power of the Supreme Court kept growing so that it was the Court that decreed the law, blocking all the bills proposed by the Right, and without restriction allowing the enactment of everything born out of the ideology of the Left, the socialists, or even communists. In the early seventies, the Supreme Court didn't object to the bill legalizing abortion, and during the years that followed kept extending the abortion law, putting the Constitutional pro-choice interpretation over pro-life rights.

Presently, a tendency to bend the Constitutional rule of the separation of Church and State can be observed in the United States. It is being twisted it in such a way that the Church will lose all influence in national and social life, and the French model of a lay state will be implemented.

It must be spelled out that pronouncing on the conformity of enacted law with the Constitution is not a purely formal procedure, nor is it a purely legal one. Wide interpretation is involved in the judgments made, which are further influenced by politics, ideology, philosophy, theology, culture, and even the legacy of a specific civilization. The judges themselves must first take account of this, so that the power entrusted to them does not give them the idea that they are some kind of high priests of democracy. They are ordinary people, placed in positions of responsibility which are defined by certain precise conditions. The nation ought to know more about these members of the Tribunal who, though not elected by general vote, wield the power to decide the fate of all of us.

The World Is Watching Us

It is worth being wary of the sophistic trick often used by journalists and politicians in an attempt to frighten common people, or possibly shaming them by statements like: "What Will the World Think of This?", "Europe Condemns Us!", "*Frankfurter Allgemeine Zeitung* Accuses Poland!", "*Le Figaro* Warns Poles!", *New York Times, Morning Star, Le Monde, Tagesblatt...* this or that.

All these are myths, metaphors and fairy tales. The world is populated by billions of people. Do all of them actually monitor what transpires in Poland on a daily basis? A great majority probably does not even know where Poland lies. As far as Europe is concerned, it is home to hundreds of millions of people who go to work in the morning, come back home tired in the evening, and if they are still able to think at all, they only think what the media tell them to think. "The world" and "Europe" are for them only what is printed in the papers, or shown on TV.

It is certain people who stand behind these media – not the world or Europe – but the owner and his hired journalists. If a publication has a large readership and a TV program a large audience, the noise they generate is great; if public interest is smaller, it is a bit calmer. But scaring people with what the world, or Europe will think is nothing more than scaring them with what the media will say.

The mechanism of intimidation is simple. In a sound community, the fear of public opinion has a positive, even desired effect. A person might do something wrong or at least shameful, but other people's opinion restrains him. Telimena, the heroine of Poland's national epic, Adam Mickiewicz's *Pan Tadeusz*, hesitates in her design to ensnare the Count. "What will the world say?" She is approaching middle age while he is young and rich. Her "world" was naturally her own people, her relatives and neighbors, the nearest and dearest. What is today's "world"? It is anonymous most of the time. We know the names of the papers, trivial as they are. *The General Paper of Frankfurt*, *The New York Times* and *The Morning Star*. Ridiculous! One would have to launch an inquiry into who the owner is and who the people writing for him are. Where does he come from and how did he make his fortune? What is his background and his policy? We know little or nothing about it. What do I know about the commentator Blauman of the *Frankfurter Allgemeine Zeitung* who shakes a warning finger at us? What is his education? Where does he get his information about Poland? Is he involved in the machinations of some lobby? We do not know this, do we? So why should we trust someone we don't know anything about? Is this supposed to be the "world" and "Europe" by which we should be cowed into submission?

Shouldn't we rather value the opinion of wise and well-meaning people who have already manifested their friendly attitude toward Poland? People who have had the chance to become familiar with our history and know that we are fighting the same battle as the West, except that theirs is virtually over, but still going on in our country? Both in Europe and North America there are very interesting academic communities, a world much more stimulating than the world of the media. Except that in the West, university professors, particularly those who do not subscribe to political correctness, have little chance of being promoted by the media, and consequently have little influence on public life. Academic life is even more disintegrated there than in Poland. In addition there is more bureaucracy to contend with. As a result, they feel rather lonely in their own schools, for which they compensate by frequent participation in various congresses and symposiums.

I know a number of American professors who keep coming to Poland "to get recharged". New York is an impressive city. But, to tell the truth, a walk down crowded streets, between skyscrapers, though overwhelming, lacks the intimacy and charm of a city that breathes the atmosphere of the past ages of history, of different epochs and styles. Only European cities exude such a climate, including Polish cities that managed to save their traditional architecture. In such surroundings, more interesting topics can be discussed than those brought up by *The New York Times*. ntelligent Americans are well aware of the mechanisms employed by the media. Finally, it was in their country that yellow journalism was born as long ago as the second half of the nineteenth century, and it was there that the media initiated their work on creating a mass audience, channeling its reactions, its way of thinking and its preferences. First, in order to promote business, then for democracy, so that free citizens would vote as the media tells them. The era of television brought about a veritable revolution, gluing entire generations to the small screen – adults and teenagers, retirees and schoolchildren – until what was on the screen became more important than real life.

In Poland, in spite of the powerful tendency to debase the mass audience, the fight is not so much for the rule of people's souls and minds, but for getting through to them. There are media that teach thinking, show ways, draw criteria, and reach out to audiences pushed into public nonexistence. It is a fascinating phenomenon, perhaps unique in the world.

To condemn the media in general is pointless. But we must differentiate, choose wisely, and act when it is reasonable so to do, when for example, we feel that our actions can serve as a counterbalance to the impudence of the media lords, moguls who would reserve the freedom of speech for themselves and usurp the role of the "world" or "Europe". We must not allow ourselves to be taken in by it. Each man is a world, and the basic question is whether it is a genuine world. The media very often do whatever they can to make this world disingenuous. But, then it is neither the world nor Europe.

The European Union – Beyond Democracy?

Democracy is not the prerequisite for a state to exist. Most political systems in world history were not democracies, but predominantly despotisms or oligarchies, that is, systems in which power was held by one individual, or by a small group of rich and cunning individuals. Democracy was a rarity.

But today democracy is in vogue. It actually came to be the ideological prerequisite, the model system obligatory in all cultures and civilizations. When Iraq was assaulted a few years back, it was for the sake of introducing democracy, no matter whether its people wanted it or not. Consequently, since then a war is being fought and there seems to be no end to it.

Russian democracy is a specific one. Since Russia had for centuries been a state ruled by the principle of absolute power, initially held by the Tsar, then by the First Secretary of the Communist Party, now, in order to be perceived by the world as a modern state, it holds allegedly democratic elections. These are arranged in such a way, however, that there is not the slightest doubt who will win.

It is the European Union, however, that has the gravest problems with democracy.

But let's read some quotations first: "There is no great share of probity necessary to support a monarchical or despotic government. The force of laws in one, and the prince's arm in the other, are sufficient to direct and maintain the whole. But in a popular state, one spring more is necessary, namely VIRTUE."

These words were written by the author considered to be the father of modern democracy. His name was Baron de Montesquieu. What idea did he convey in the cited fragment of his 1748 treatise *The Spirit of the Laws* (III, 3)? The fact that despotism is easy, and democracy difficult. Despotism is easy because it's easier to rule a state when everything is in one hand: the legislation, the judiciary, and the government. No one will murmur, no one has the right or authority to protest, and the ruler can do everything. Thus the state is strong, has a powerful army and efficient economy. But there is one problem: the people. Are they free, or are they slaves? If they are slaves, can they be happy?

Democracy is difficult, because for it to work, those who rule must know how to share power and not confuse lawmaking with governing, and both with the judiciary. What's more, they must abide by a suitably high moral standard, since this is what the word "virtue" means. Montesquieu bluntly ridicules the English who got rid of a despotic government in order to introduce democracy. All for nothing as: "At length, when the country had undergone the most violent shocks, they were obliged to have recourse to the very government which they had so wantonly proscribed." This happened because of the lack of moral principles, because the power was seized by quarreling individuals blinded by ambition and envy.

Montesquieu writes: "The politic Greeks, who lived under a popular government, knew no other support than virtue. The modern inhabitants of that country are entirely taken up with manufacture, commerce, finances, opulence, and luxury." He further warns: "When virtue is banished, ambition invades the minds of those who are disposed to receive it, and avarice possesses the whole community."

It is exactly like this today, as though Montesquieu were witnessing things contemporary politicians tend to resort to, turning democracy into an absurdity and into its own caricature. So many of these politicians would burst out laughing upon hearing the word "virtue."

But it is none other than Montesquieu whom present-day champions of democracy invoke. However, it is doubtful whether they ever examined his work, or even read as much as the sections concerning democracy.

So let us keep reading: "As virtue is necessary in a republic, and in a monarchy honor, so FEAR is necessary in a despotic government" (III, 9). What politician talks about virtue nowadays, or about honor? For what politician will moral principles always precede enacted law? There is no virtue nor honor today. There is only a proliferation of regulations, not by thousands anymore, but by hundreds of thousands.

These laws are not enacted by a parliament whose essential prerogative in a democratic system is lawmaking. No, the European Union relegates parliament to the role of a chamber in which deputies, extravagantly remunerated, can just talk according to the etymology of the term "parliament" (from the Latin word *"parlare"* – "to talk"). Actual laws are enacted by the European Commission and the Council of Ministers, whose members are elected in a totally undemocratic way, and an average citizen of a member state of the Union has no idea whatsoever who the individuals serving on these bodies are. No wonder then that in the Union people are first of all being intimidated. We are being threatened with numerous penalties if we do not abide by this, or that rule enacted by the high commissioners. The specter of penalty becomes more and more the frequent tool of government.

If so, however, this is no longer democracy. These are methods from the repertoire of a despotic system, so lucidly described by the father of modern democracy, Baron de Montesquieu.

Since the European Union is still in the process of defining its rules, aims and means, we must keep reacting astutely and boldly to its diverse experiments leading to the inevitable collapse of the great heritage of European civilization, including the treasure of democracy.

That is why the so-called Lisbon Treaty must not be implemented without the unanimous approval of all member states in referendums, so that democracy can be saved from the despotism of technocrats. Europe cannot be appropriated by them. Europe is our heritage, and we have an absolute right to preserve the democratic and Christian character of this heritage.

Let's Look at the Media

Present-day democracy makes us once more ponder the dilemma that has loomed large in the minds of philosophers for hundreds, if not thousands of years: what is more important, reason or will? This dilemma is very clearly reflected in the post-election syndrome, which might be informally called moral hangover. Should voting be merely an act of individual freedom of exercising one's civil rights, or is it as important to know who one is voting for, or in other words, not only to act freely, but also reasonably, as a person informed about the truth. Present-day democracy, unfortunately, has been about 99 percent appropriated by the media, and as a result, although we exercise our freedom of choice, for most voters it has become an issue secondary to whether they really, truly know for whom and for what program they are voting. They let themselves be led by the nose, they mistake the chaff for the grain and empty promises for the real thing. Well, no use wasting more breath! So what should we do? We must study the media! In order for a democracy to remain a democracy, not a mere object of manipulation, that voters be treated as serious citizens, not as dimwits, the study of the media must be introduced as an obligatory subject beginning in elementary schools.

So let's highlight a few seemingly commonplace rules. Television is, of course, the most persuasive medium. But we must remember that TV is a screen first, not a loudspeaker, and consequently what counts most is picture, not voice. This means that when watching a political program, the audience pays attention not to what is being said, but to the totality of the take. Therefore it is not the precision of the argument that matters, but rather where the speaker is seated, whether it is on the left or on the right, or perhaps too far left or right.

Inches matter in the proportions of the screen! Politicians, upon entering the studio, sit where they are told. They concentrate on what they are going to say, perhaps trying to remember as well that they must smile from time to time. They are not aware that, by making them sit here or there, social engineering specialists have already positioned them according to their hidden political agenda. These are vital matters in the crucial hours of an election campaign. That is why a decent Rightist electoral committee must have its own expert who not only listens, but knows how to read the screen, sees when the odds have been stacked against them, and sounds the alarm bell immediately. While watching the debate, moreover, he'd better turn off the sound completely as the speakers' arguments can be better assessed then. Not from the point of view of what was said, but of how it might have influenced the audiences. And this is the first rule.

The second rule is to know whom one is actually addressing. Is it the anchorperson, one's supporters, one's adversaries, or the disengaged? It is crucial for the verbal part, because different arguments must be used addressing the first, the second and the third group. If those listening are my supporters, they are likely to vote for me anyway, what matters for them is that I am self-assured and strengthen their convictions. If the listeners are my adversaries, they will be hard to convince, unless their likings can be somehow undermined and not necessarily by a factual argument.

We must remember that in political debates there is a counterargument for each argument. This is usually monitored by a board of advisers. "If he tells you that the problem of unemployment has been solved as the percentage of the employed has significantly grown, you answer that it is because our poor youngsters had to leave the country in search of work." Such an exchange can be continued indefinitely because this argument will be countered by the argument that these youngsters left poor and will come back rich, with saved money and a wealth of experience, thus making the country richer. It is also important at which point the anchor cuts in on a ping-pong of arguments, since he or she can do it precisely when this or that debater has the upper hand.

There is no way to fight preferences. We had a president (ex-communist) known to have an alcohol problem. This didn't prevent him from being elected twice, and with a great majority (especially the second time). Many voters ignored the fact that, intoxicated, he staggered at the graves of the Polish officers murdered by the Soviets, or tried to enter his car through the trunk. Voters were simply fond of him. But it appears that he had no mean predecessors. It is said that Winston Churchill himself, Prime Minister of Great Britain and a national hero, "drank like a fish," and even used drugs (presumably to bolster up his courage). What's more, he was capricious, stubborn, rude, unpredictable and hard to get along with. Yet in spite of all of this Lord Alanbrooke thanked God that he had the privilege of working and spending time with him, considering him a superman walking this earth (D. Ogilvy, *Confessions of an Advertising Man*, New York, 1971, p. 23).

This just shows that political preferences of the general public are ruled by a mysterious logic which seldom coincides with virtue, wisdom or *raison d'état*. These preferences may change from one election to the next. It is the party that happens to guess these in advance that will win, even if they lie 'through their teeth.

It may sound like a paradox, but the expansion of the media, supposedly the means of public communication, results in removing us from reality in more and more devious ways. The message is distorted by manipulation, reason is put to sleep, and the act of choosing is reduced to a behavioral, statistical reaction. Thus, in order to save our freedom, we must apply reason, be wary of the media and able to remain in touch with reality. Remember, unreasonable freedom is no freedom.

Soviet Propaganda

Much has been said and written about the German propaganda machine headed by Dr. Joseph Goebbels. Indeed, the method of handling information applied by that undoubtedly intelligent though evil individual was effective. However, the Soviet propaganda machine was also very effective, it was created earlier and its leaders, men like Trotsky, Zinoviev and Radek, were no mediocrities. What's more, the effective methods of Soviet propaganda, perhaps because so seldom highlighted, have survived and prosper to this very day.

Communism, masquerading as a "scientific ideology" (what an absurd clash of ideas), made a wide use of scholarship and was especially fond of sociology and psychology. The masses, to be effectively controlled, must be thoroughly studied and that is the purpose of sociology and psychology. A mass of people resembles one body, except that its reactions are different from those of a single human being. So scholarly research must describe and foresee these reactions.

The proletariat was to be the society of the future, the new "chosen people", but not to be ignored was the fact that it continued to be impressed by the "loathsome" world of the aristocracy, by the good life of the residents of palaces, by their magnificent balls and elegant clothes. Theirs was the life of its dreams. Propaganda experts knew these dreams and knew that they had to be fed. Since the palaces had been plundered during the very first years of the revolution and famine was plagued everyday life, how was this to be done? The answer wasn't that complicated. It lay in the world of dreams incarnated in art. So theaters kept operating, and the better part of the tickets was distributed among the proletarians. For free. But what was produced? Plays extolling the revolution and communism? Far from it! Professor Charles Sarolea, a Belgian scholar, wrote in his 1924 *Impressions of Soviet Russia*: "When one thought of the subjects of most of the operas, ballets and the dramas, one could not help being struck by the curious paradox that the audiences were transported every night from their Bolshevist surroundings into an aristocratic world of heroic kings and gallant knights of romance and chivalry" (pp. 13-14).

It was a paradox indeed, not an absurd one, though, but one precisely premeditated. Several decades later, the very same stratagem was employed in Poland under communist rule. Naturally, the hits of TV programs then were not Soviet, but American movies that nourished the dreams of mass audiences about the West, this new paradise on earth. When shown, however, such films were always screened in combination with Soviet and anti-American propaganda. Between one film and the next, news or political commentaries were aired, preaching that capitalism was inferior to communism, and arguing that the Soviet Union was a peace-loving country, and it was imperialist America that presented a threat to the world. The same principle was employed on the regime radio, especially on its Program 1. Anti-Western propaganda was interspersed there with American musical hits from the top of current lists. The programmers were well aware that if they were to broadcast Soviet music, songs extolling Stalin, Brezhnev or Andropov, all their efforts would be to no avail.

How did the propagandists discover this paradox? Scholarly observation taught them that the psychological structure of mass audiences is far from logical, that "human beasts" lack coherence and consequence. Thus, in order to achieve the desired effect, they must be fed contradictions, emotionally highly-charged contradictions. Masses like to love and hate the same thing, and at the same time.

No wonder then that during the early years after the revolution, when the new art of cinema became popular, Soviet proletarians were shown mostly American movies. Wasn't it likewise in the Polish People's Republic? There were long lines for American films, tickets were always in short supply and could often be obtained only at exorbitant prices from scalpers. Why such generous presentation of the hated capitalist productions?

Because before every show viewers had to willy-nilly absorb a great dose of communist propaganda in the form of a newsreel screened in the darkness of a large auditorium, a hypnotic séance. That's all there was to it!

Soviet propaganda was only partly of national origin. Sarolea asserts that "the methods of Bolshevist agitation and propaganda are a poisonous mixture, in varying doses, of the new methods of American yellow journalism with the old methods of Tsarism". And he explains: "And those two different methods are represented by two different types of men. The first type, which is the dominant one, is the type of American-Russian Jew who has learnt his trade on the other side of the Atlantic. The second type, who prefers to keep discreetly in the background, or even more discreetly to work underground, is the former Tsarist official, the 'Agent Provocateur', or the spy, who has transferred his services from the pre-war Intelligence Department to the Soviet Foreign Office" (pp. 107-108).

Thus Soviet propaganda was a peculiar blend of methods borrowed from journalistic and advertising practices already well established across the Ocean, in the free world of the so vilified capitalism and the operating methods of the functionary-informer-spy circles, whose cadres and practices were inherited from the tsarist regime, which though as much vilified as capitalism, were nevertheless just as useful.

So what is the situation today? Has much changed in Poland in this respect? It is worthwhile to watch closely the way in which most of our media function, the people who run them, and their operating methods that, even though nominally different, are a direct continuation of the practices of the old Soviet school. Who can tell if the ideological fragmentation of Polish society isn't the result of the very same kind of propaganda, coming from the same communist circles? There are numerous indications that this is so. If it is so, we must avoid such media like the plague. Let them operate for themselves. We must have our own media that would be national in spirit.

A Bit of Wisdom

Hardly anybody nowadays can complain of having time 'to kill'; what is really common instead, is a lack of time. We are constantly on the go, rushing from one place to the next, having to attend to innumerable matters hanging over our heads like clouds. Everything must be taken care of instantly, this very minute. We don't talk to one another, we just exchange meaningless words, we don't read consciously, just glance at a text, we are even unable to rest decently. Short disrupted sleep. A few days of vacation. Eternal nerves, stresses...

The world has changed. There was once an epoch without cars, planes, phones, electricity, Internet, without all those things that make life easier, shorten distances and save time. But in spite of all these conveniences we lack time. Real time. The Roman philosopher, Lucius Annaeus Seneca, wrote about it as much as two thousand years ago: "When people try to argue that a pressing business stands between them and the pursuit of liberal culture, don't believe them: they're shamming busy, exaggerating, busying themselves willfully" (*Letters to Lucilius*, LXII, 1). It's exactly the same when we ask adults today what they read, when and for how long. The usual answer is: "I don't read anything, I don't have time, I'm too busy. All I can manage is watching the news, glancing at the headlines in the papers or on internet. That's it".

We have forgotten the wise way of spending leisure time that once characterized the Western civilisations of Greece, of Rome and of Christianity: the way most befitting supposedly free people, the way that centuries ago was known in Poland as "sedulous idleness", consisted mostly in reading, or pursuing one's own creativity (*otia litterata*); it could also be a meeting of people who had things to say to one another. Today, a meeting usually means a general hubbub, i.e. everybody speaking at the same time, without rhyme or reason, shouting, noise, and a general din. Or, otherwise, there is silence, dead silence, and bleak gloom. Healthy humor has also been lost; what prevails are malicious witticisms, or outright vulgarisms. All this as a result of people no longer knowing how to focus their thoughts before speaking and only then sharing ththoughts with others.

Seneca wrote: "No man of exalted character enjoys the low and mean: it's the vision of greatness that summons and uplifts him" (*Letters to Lucilius*, XXXIX, 2). What is it that people talk about today? It is degrading to listen. They talk about nothing, or about things low and mean, adapting their language to the subject matter to boot. These are conversations encouraged, or outright inspired by the media of the gender that used to be known as gutter journalism, although gutters might appear to be of immaculate white marble in comparison.

These complaints are not cheap moralizing. We have a serious problem. We must aspire to things great and profound in our lifetime. We cannot just pursue eternal youth, which might be attractive but pointless. Nor can we passively succumb to the course of time, wilting like leaves. In order for our souls to open to grand things, they need cultivation, which is impossible without our exerting ourselves, without words of encouragement, without fortifying friendship. A human being must grow. And vital among life's goals is a proper filling of our leisure time when we can consciously separate things important from marginal, and concentrate our loving concern on people worth devoting our time to and spending it with them. Our being finds fulfillment then, even if it is time spared, often stolen from the excess of matters entrapping us, thwarting what's most beautiful, which we all too frequently allow to happen.

Without great literature, man gropes in the dark. But mass media tickle the vanity of the culturally ignorant, making them believe that they know and understand everything because they have read twenty newspaper headlines and five articles. It is of such pap that opinion is born. But what is this kind of opinion worth? Seneca answers: "Opinion disregards truth; a better opinion has he who deserves worse and the better man has a worse one" (*Phaedra*, verses 269-270). All this is rubbish steeped in scorn, envy and spite: an intellectually bottomless void.

Under democracy, not much can be prohibited, so papers financed by foreign capital will continue being published, deviously disparaging Poles and their culture; anti-Catholic publications will continue appearing; movies showing people degraded to the level of beasts will continue being produced. But should we pay one cent for things like this? Must we devote one second of our time to them? Why? What for? The answer is simple. We do because we do not understand! Seneca explained: "We have made our world into darkness. We're quite blind; we never see whether a thing is good or bad for us. All our life we are bumping into things, but that never makes us pull up or tread more warily" (*Letters to Lucilius*, CX, 7). Oh, human nature, one would like to exclaim, have you not changed in two thousand years?

Still! We read such texts and it dawns on us. It has all happened before. But now we recognize it, so we are not doomed. But this places on us a great deal of responsibility. So let us learn to try to live differently. Let us be a bit wiser at the least.

Had it Been a Pole…

Soccer is definitely the king of team sports. Soccer games bring tens of thousands of spectators to the stadiums, and there are games watched by tens of millions on TV. This was the case of the 2006 World Cup finals.

For us boys growing up in Poland, soccer brings a boyhood memory of games played on some stretch of grassland, with carelessly lined T-shirts marking the goal, its bar only imagined. We chased the ball, laughing our heads off when someone managed to feign a scoring pass, and throwing tantrums when a score was denied, even though the ball evidently flew under the bar. Also fondly remembered are the seventies when some of our national team players earned such fame that soccer fans in France, the United States and even Madagascar can name them up to this day. And now? Now we hear that soccer teams buy players for as much as 40 million Euros. As though it were white slave traffic, only with prices thousand times the price ever paid for any slave in the history of the world. The difference is that these men are not forced to play and they don't play for nothing. They have a chance of becoming millionaires. Neither are spectators forced to watch a game, either. So what's the problem?

It is the shameless performance of soccer game commentators. We suddenly hear that the man with the clean-shaven head and his entire body covered with tattoos, who has just hit his opponent so hard that the latter fell and is writhing in pain, that this man is not only a great player, but an idol, an outright hero whom we are supposed to admire and presumably imitate. At this point, the act of watching the game proves to have been a miscalculation, and following its development further would turn into a nightmare. The players trip and push one another, tear at their opponents' shirts, viciously elbow their ribs, kick even their faces, spit left and right, sometimes at their own teammates, and all this to the applause of the audience and raves of the commentators. Any moment we expect to hear exhortations: "Hit him so that he won't get up, trample on him, break his bones!" Soccer has become so brutal and dishonest (corrupt), that it has ended up far removed from the ethos of a genuine sport, and from its own history.

One can condone the fact that some people make huge profits from it. Mass audiences absorb ads like air, unaware that some brand name, some picture flashed in front of their eyes during a game will invade their subconscious, augmenting the clientele, increasing the profits of the tycoons of world markets. But why should soccer players be presented as models to be imitated, as national heroes? Well, sports commentators and politicians depend upon mass audiences. Their livelihood depends on them, so they have to play up to them and react in this way. Naturally, it won't be the heads of state who would be cheering or jeering like plebeians once did in the Roman Colosseum. Why would they? Because the ball just missed the goal? But roaring crowds have become the mark of present-day democracy, so they have to be courted. "We are just like you, our dear audience, esteemed viewers, cherished soccer fans". And subliminally: "Elect us once more. By voting for us you vote for yourselves".

The system sagged when Zidane suddenly turned, approached his opponent and butted his chest so vehemently that the latter somersaulted. A moment of horror ensued: this from a hero, the player of the century, and even an *arbiter elegantiarum*. But the dismay didn't last long. An explanation was soon found. Zidane, like many a player defending the honor of France, is an Algerian, so surely the opposing Italian must have provoked the hero by throwing some racial slur at him. It must have upset him so greatly that, as a man of honor, he couldn't restrain himself and gave the Italian a taste of his own medicine. Bent his head and struck the culprit's rib cage. And the Italian obligingly fell, for it pays to fall, and more and more soccer players get to be fall artists. So much so that an average viewer has a hard time catching on to whether the fall resulted from a real foul or was just a feat of deliberate acrobatics. True, Zidane had to leave the field momentarily, but he has long since absolved, the unfortunate incident buried in oblivion, negligible in view of his long-standing service for the national colors of France. So the idol was restored to his pedestal.

Discussing the incident, a friend of mine wondered what would have been the reaction if a Pole behaved like this. Can you imagine what would ensue? Can you visualize the headlines? Can you hear the comments? "Brutal Foul by Pole", "Poland Discredited", "Poles Worse than Nazis", "Polish Xenophobia", etc. There would be no excuse for such behavior by a Polish soccer player. Not only would he be blamed, but the entire nation. The entire country would be called to account for the last thousand years, and the coming thousand years for good measure. This is the way smear campaigns against our country are orchestrated by the media all over the world, accompanied by some Polish-language papers in our country. So perhaps it was fortunate, after all, that our team did not make the World Cup finals. Because one of our players might also have lost his temper upon hearing (hearing because he would have read it in the German tabloids over and over again) that he comes from a country of thieves and drunks.

Soccer has completely lost its sporting and educational dimension; it has slid into the dimension of economic-political events, even ideological ones. And, after the last World Cup, for many of us it may have become a memory not worth returning to.

Homo-manipulation

Homosexuality is one of the subjects closely monitored by the censorship of political correctness. Most public figures are scared stiff of the subject, especially media people and politicians, and if forced to voice their opinion on it, they resort to generalizations so that no one would be offended. Naturally, there are also persons who have the promotion of "sexual minorities" as part of their ideological agenda as a means of boosting their political capital. They are, conversely, insistent, often aggressive and provocative in their declarations. It is a sensitive subject, no doubt, abundant in traps, as the rights of sexual minorities (mostly referred to as "sexual orientations" in the media nowadays) are more and more frequently included in the package of human rights. Homosexuality must no longer be described as a perversion or deviation, because it would be considered discrimination, an act of "homophobia", a violation of a human right threatened by lawsuits and punishment.

It is significant that the problem, instead of being clearly named, is being hidden behind the screen of Greek and Latin words. It is deplorable, because this allows for manipulation already on the linguistic level, as very few of us know Greek and Latin nowadays. So let's decode the manipulation.

People who forewarn about the negative consequences of homosexuality are called "homophobes". The word seems to be a Latin-Greek conglomerate, which it isn't. "Phobia" means "fear" in Greek. And "homo"? One might naturally understand it as meaning a human being, and would be right if it were Latin, as "homo" means just this in Latin. "Homophobia" would then be a fear of human beings. A terrible allegation. One must be a friend of human beings, not their detractor. People who warn against homosexuality, who discern something morally wrong and reprehensible about it, would in this (erroneous) interpretation be enemies of the human race. Unimaginable. But the "homo" component of such words as "homophobia" and "homosexuality" is not of Latin, but of Greek origin. And in Greek "homos" does not denote a human being, but a thing of the same kind, something alike, as in the word "homogenous". So what does it really amount to? Homosexuality means a relation between two individuals of the same sex, and homophobia means a fear of such (homosexual) relations, both on moral and religious grounds; it in no way means fear of the human race as such. We must fear evil things, evil is objectionable, harmful and horrible. Children and young people must be protected from evil as they easily succumb to manipulation. While respecting all people as human beings, we must be wary, as some of them are liars, thieves, even murderers. The Earth is not a paradise, and people are not little angels. Not all of them anyway.

It is a widespread misconception that the cradle of European homosexuality was Greece, with Plato as its major figure. Since the Greeks laid the foundations of Western Civilization with its culture of the highest order, why should something associated with this heritage be censured? However, this is also manipulation. This myth has been dispelled by Dr. Marek Czachorowski in his reliable and illuminating book whose English title would read *Heterophobia, Homosexuality and the Greek Roots of Europe*, published in Tychy (Poland) in 2006. What's more, this writer shows that the manipulation invaded even some translations of Plato's dialogues. Thus, when Socrates, this unequaled paragon of wisdom, as well as a righteous and courageous man, hears from Callicles that "a man who is going to live a full life must allow his desires to become as mighty as may be and never repress them" (*Gorgias*, 492), he demonstrates, applying his customary method of a series of rhetorical questions, that such life would be "dreadful, ugly and wretched" (Ibid., 494). But whose life? Indeed! Socrates uses the word "*kinaidos*". The Polish translator, Władysław Witwicki, following the suggestion of writer Gabriela Zapolska, interprets it as... "leopard", i.e. "*lampart*" in Polish.

But why should a leopard lead a dreadful, ugly and wretched life, we wonder. Because he scratches indecently? And why a leopard in the first place? Why not a tiger, a lion or a coyote?

78

Well, during the nineteenth century the word "*lampart*" was used in Polish in the now forgotten, secondary meaning of a debauched man, a rake. But Dr. Czachorowski points out that the Greek-Polish dictionary defines the word "*kinaidos*" as meaning not just a man who indulges in debauchery in general, but one given to debauchery of an unnatural kind. It is not what the Polish word "*lampart*" indicates. Władysław Witwicki, seemingly uneasy about calling a spade a spade, violated the original text which he should on no account have done. It wasn't a matter of selecting the right word, a situation frequently faced by translators. He may have disagreed with the opinions of his author, but he wasn't free to clearly falsify the text. It was just fraud. And committed when? He translated the dialogue in 1922, almost a century ago, so already then political correctness spread its tentacles to constrain seemingly intelligent people.

Besides terms like "homophobia", there are also terms such as "pedophilia" and "zoophilia". The latter perversions (deviations) have not been legitimized as of now, but they gradually enter the public domain, initially suggested in ads. Their exponents cautiously check the ground, sound it out, awaiting an opportunity to push us from the paved (moral) road into the morass of deviation. If no one objects, they will push more and more forcefully, until they achieve their aim.

The sources of our culture are not poisoned. There are many invigorating streams. Ancient Greeks knew how to discern between good and evil, so let us listen to Socrates. He knew what he was saying, was not afraid of even dying for the truth inconvenient to the powers that be. This was because he was a true philosopher and loved wisdom, which cannot exist without righteousness.

Disciples of the Encyclopedists

It seems that some unknown body, no doubt consisting of advocates of democracy and freedom of speech, decreed that Radio Maryja and its Director, Father Dr. Tadeusz Rydzyk, must be ceaselessly tormented, that charges – any old charges – must be constantly put forward against them, that they must be harassed, plagued, defamed, vilified, slandered without end, and then harassed, plagued, defamed again... It must be a highly enlightened group of people because they strictly follow the rules worked out by the authors of the Great French *Encyclopedia*, who propagated the cult of reason and freedom, including the freedom of speech. The first condition for speech to be free is the abolition of censorship. No wonder then that d'Alembert and Diderot preached against the royal censorship which was "oppressive" in their opinion (see *Censorship in Wielkopolska under Prussian Occupation 1815-1914* by G. Kucharczyk, Poznań 2001, p. 16). Publicly, they contended that every country would fall into "stupidity, prejudice and superstition" if its people were not allowed to think according to their will, and write what they thought. That was why censorship had to be abolished. But privately they harbored different opinions. Censorship was to remain... to monitor the critics of their bosom child, the *Encyclopedia* – texts criticizing it had to be unconditionally confiscated. Not only did they think so, but d'Alembert and Diderot actually submitted such a petition to the King's minister. The minister turned it down, which, as one memoirist testifies, was met by d'Alembert's fit of rage and swearing ("which was his bad habit").

What we are witnessing today in Poland is the rebirth of the mentality of those learned men of the Enlightenment. Freedom of speech, press, radio, television, yes, but for us! Whoever is against us, will be censored, banned, fired, imprisoned... And to begin with, his good name will be dragged through the mud, his opinions branded as obscurantism.

The media rhetoric of these circles is not very sophisticated, relying mostly on the short memory or inferior education of the general public, whom they flatter and woo as the genuine elite. Tolerance, in its postmodernist version especially, is pure fiction as shown just by these continuing irrational and tasteless attacks on Radio Maryja. But they are a sign of an incredible impotence as well, and we wonder what kind of paper tigers people standing behind these attacks are. They make a great racket with their headlines, videos, photo/audio montages, but they won't show their faces, appear in public and announce: "I am so and so, and I accuse this or that person!" They hide behind one another, behind a headline or title. They put on various masks, pretend to be God knows who, but they would tear the victim apart while still alive. It smacks of what the Austrian minister, Prince von Metternich, said about German journalists some hundred and fifty years ago: "Most of them are superficially educated students, dismissed public officials, writers without a publisher, bankrupt speculators". That was why he hoped his nation wouldn't fall so low as to consider them "the galaxy of moral paragons" (Ibid., p. 28). Let's hope that our nation won't fall so low, either, and won't lend its ear to all those calumnies coming from extremely strange sources and even stranger circles.

And what would we say to these words? "If you assembled all the newspaper publishers enjoying freedom of speech in one place, you would have a gathering to whom you wouldn't entrust your pet dog, let alone your honor and reputation" (Ibid., p. 29). Strong words indeed! We wonder if today any public person would dare utter such words in fear of a consolidated counter-attack of media personages who would consider themselves to have been "hurt", "offended" and "insulted". Does it mean that we shouldn't cite the words uttered by the Belgian king, Leopold I, as long ago as 1836? Well, we are citing them, especially since these words were not uttered publicly, but privately, to the future Queen of England. It is worth noting that the media was only the press at the time, there was no radio or television, and the press as an incipient mass medium already manifested what it was capable of. Rational people, conscious of their dignity and integrity, saw what was and would continue to happen because of the omnipotence of the press. The reality certainly surpassed their expectations, but their intuitions turned out to be right.

Work in the media is exceptionally demanding. Most people so engaged simply do not meet this requirement in terms of the necessary knowledge, education and talent. It is not manufacturing the gun, but it is frequently pulling the trigger. A rather simple act, but one must ask oneself who one is shooting at. Who gave me the right to shoot? Am I to follow all the publisher's orders?

These are the questions all media people must ask themselves, and answer them not only in accordance with the code of journalistic ethics, but also in harmony with their own conscience.

The "Face" of an Animal

Nature films are tools of a large-scale propaganda of evolutionism, propaganda more and more frequently implemented by means of language, i.e. the use of particular terms. Left-wing (Marxist) ideology worked out by the philosophers of the so-called Frankfurt School for the Western world, which triumphs today in democratic societies where everything is permitted and nothing can be forbidden.

Even this, however, is not so certain, as quite recently the European Council introduced a ban on teaching creationism. Only evolutionism may be taught. One wonders how it can be reconciled with Article 13 of the Charter of Fundamental Rights of the European Union which reads: "The arts and scientific research shall be free of constraint. Academic freedom shall be respected". But it appears that establishing a law is not enough, what counts is its interpretation, and this is a delicate matter. Evidently the European Council knows best what should be permitted and what should not. A pity, though, that the pertinent restriction hasn't been included in the Charter of Fundamental Rights. The situation would be clearer then. On the other hand, if creationism, i.e. the fact that man was created by God, should be banned, how can Christians, Muslims and Jews approve of a Charter that undermines this basic dogma of their creed?

Let us acquaint ourselves with the justification for the ban on teaching creationism. It turns out that creationism poses a threat to human rights and democracy. "Heavenly Mother!", one would like to exclaim. Has the European Council lost its mind to embrace such nonsense? Isn't it precisely creationism that which guarantees human rights as it considers man an intelligent and free being, created in God's own image. Were it not for the tenets of intelligence and freedom there would be no question of human rights at all. How would a man devoid of intelligence know that he had any rights, even if he had some?

How could he demand that his rights be respected if he had no free will? It is intelligence and free will which prove that man originates from God and not from inanimate matter. Matter doesn't think, or wish for it has no such faculties. Neither plants, nor even animals, think or wish, even though the latter have a rich sensory and emotional life. But they have no intellectual or volitional life.

Preaching freedom while stripping man of intelligence and reducing him to the level of an animal means either a lack of logic, or complete ignorance. Somebody might assert that man does not differ from animals, from apes, goats or sheep. So it seems to him, so he thinks, so he presumes. It's his right. But surmising this, he acts as a thinking creature, whereas apes, goats or sheep don't consider themselves humans. Why? Because they don't think. This is the difference between us and the animal world. A man, even when expressing the strangest, the most absurd ideas, behaves like a human being because eccentricity (not to call it outright stupidity) is also a function of thought, and an attribute of man only. Even his atypical whims are clearly human, because animal behavior is always typical. A tiger won't venture onto the ocean, to go whaling. A donkey won't try to reach the moon, and even in the longest process of evolution, they won't reach the stage that would make them aspire to these things. Whereas man goes whaling and has landed on the moon.

What kind of people make up the European Council? What inspires their intellects to utter such an irrational concept? Not irrational in that they preach evolutionism, but in the fact that, while preaching freedom of speech and learning, they thereby limit freedom of speech and learning. It is the greatest absurdity imaginable, considering that it comes from the Council of Europe, a body made up of Council of Ministers (forty-seven foreign ministers and their deputies), a Parliamentary Assembly (636 members), a Congress of Local and Regional Authorities of the European Council, and a Secretariat (1,800 persons). Altogether this amounts to about 2,500 people. One would like to say: the elite of the elites. But is it really?

Getting public opinion accustomed to the language of evolutionism involves describing the animal kingdom in human terms. Animals have faces, even though they used to have snouts. A lioness has two daughters and one son. Daughters wonder where their mother has gone, and the son misses his cousins because he would like to share with them the excitement of Momma's having brought an antelope. Papa wonders whether to go north or south, and finally goes west, which seems the best option to secure an evening meal for his wife and progeny.

You listen and cannot believe your ears. You see something totally different from what the melodious female voice of the TV commentator tells you. It is like a trance. You see a huge lion snout and bloodshot eyes, merciless fangs and a dull head bent only on killing, gobbling up prey and sleeping. A beast that nurses creatures of the same ilk, too. But the lady on the screen is of a different opinion; she treats the beast as a human. But since this is possible only on film, not in the real world, maybe she really wants to turn man into animal, as we are all cousins: apes, pigs and humans.

There are people who miss guidance and/or some new ideology after the fall of bloodthirsty communism. To fill the void, they developed a belief in evolutionism. This is to be the new ideology of the Left, or rather their new religion, as it has been decreed from above, to replace creationism.

Let's be weary of these people. They pose a real threat if they don't know the difference between a snout and a face, between animal and man, between an object and a person.

Blurring such vital differences always led to totalitarianism. That is why it isn't creationism, but evolutionism which should be prohibited, if human rights are supposed to mean the rights of each person.

An Unpunished Crime

The formation of a national elite is a long process. It takes many generations of citizens who know their goal, who cherish tradition and set their sights on the well-being and development of the nation they come from. It may happen that a natural talent, a real gem, emerges, but he or she has a chance to excel only if noticed, appreciated and guided by someone wise and well-meaning. Many talents are lost because there is no one to nurture them. Others, though they rise high, flourish only for themselves, without benefitting their nation. Usually most people are of average abilities, which doesn't prevent them from taking advantage of the achievements of outstanding individuals. Thus one needn't be a Chopin in order to enjoy his Polonaises, or an Edison in order to benefit from his having invented a light bulb.

Among the important members of the national elite are men of learning, notably those who reached the highest level of knowledge, i.e. university professors. Already in antiquity there were renowned academies, e.g. Plato's Academy or Aristotle's Lyceum. Later, during the Middle Ages, when universities came into being, the tradition of these ancient sages was continued by professors, then called magisters. Today, professors stand higher in the hierarchy than doctors (PhDs) or masters (MAs). Of course they are engaged in teaching, but only after they have themselves studied for long years, and, in fact, they keep studying all their lives.

In the centuries when Poland did not exist as a state, being partitioned among Russia, Prussia and Austria, our scholars often worked outside their country, since the prerequisite for scholarship is freedom which was then nonexistent in their subjugated fatherland. But when Poland regained independence after the First World War, many of them came back, considering it their moral duty. One of them was Tadeusz Zieliński, the world famous authority on Greek and Roman civilizations.

Universities such as the Stefan Batory University of Wilno or Jan Kazimierz University of Lwów were brought back to their former splendor, and new ones were founded, such as KUL, the Catholic University of Lublin. A community of scholars was reborn, specialists in some fields gained international fame, like the renowned Polish school of logic. But soon the new war came, and Polish scholarship was suppressed. Not only were school and university buildings destroyed, but high school teachers and university professors became the target of repression.

Occupiers, both German and Soviet, acted systematically, according to plan. Well in advance, informants and traitors helped them prepare proscription lists with names and addresses of people who were to be arrested, repressed and even killed. Knowledgeable people and patriots had always been a threat to conquerors and occupiers. The occupiers were now bent on proving that the Polish nation was dumb, uneducated and unfit to govern itself. How could it be best proven? By imprisoning the well-educated, and eventually killing them off. Yes, killing them off!

Here we come to the heart of our national tragedy. Our professors were imprisoned, silenced and slaughtered with premeditation. Yes, with premeditation. In cold blood. With the logic of individuals considering themselves supermen, people not bound by any moral principles in dealing with creatures of a lower order.

One might argue that this happened a long time ago. Why bring it up? Well, this was at once long ago and not so long ago since, we are suffering from the consequences to this very day. In place of the genuine elite of the old professors, the communist regime produced hundreds if not thousands of masqueraders in various domains of our life, universities included. The fear manifested by academics when recently confronted with the prospect of having to undergo a vetting procedure was a telltale spectacle. On the other hand, the same communist regime of yesterday did not see fit to demand justice for the slaughter of our professors. No one in authority then was the least interested. Consequently, very few people today realize that no one was punished or even brought before the court for the murder of twenty-two Polish professors of the Lwów University, although the murderer was actually known. It was one Hans Krüger who himself admitted the fact to Professor Karolina Lanckorońska when he expected her also to be executed shortly. But Professor Lanckorońska survived. She wrote about it later, but her testimony was ignored until she was called to appear in court in Münster on April 28, 1967, to testify against Krüger. But when she started her account of the murder of the Polish professors, she was cut short by the presiding judge who was not interested in this crime. Why? Because it was the case of the Jews murdered in the town of Stanisławów. Professor Lanckorońska didn't allow herself be silenced, though, and related everything she knew about the murder of the Polish professors.

It came as a shock to many listeners who had been unaware of it. Then somebody raised the question of why it was that only she who spoke about it. Why wasn't the matter raised by Polish authorities? It was unimaginable that a crime of this magnitude should be officially ignored. But it was. And although Krüger was eventually sentenced, it was not for the murder of the Polish professors [see: S. Bogdanowicz, "The Life and Work of Karolina Lanckorońska" in *The Bulletin of the Institute of National Remembrance*, no. 3 (74) of March 2007]. Such was the Polish People's Republic, its authorities and its professors in all their glory! Absolutely no interest! Dead silence!

If we want to rehabilitate our elites, the academic ones in particular, we must keep returning to the past. It is a past that is not so distant, either. It is still troubled by the memories of people striving to reclaim justice and the rights they deserve.

Simulated Debates

It is a sad fact that our national media, television in particular, resorts to manipulation as it did under communism. The old staff and their methods remained. They are seasoned workers, and, as such, all the more dangerous. They know how to operate in the changed conditions, and how to cope even with pluralism of opinion. To avoid the charge of one-sidedness, television presents different opinions, some supporting an idea, some opposing it. It is seemingly all right, but at close scrutiny, one sees the delicate and deliberate hand of the manipulator. He's vigilant, he doesn't even mind pluralism.

It is because of the manipulators' persistence that common types of simulated, or "bogus" debates and arguments are worth exposing for the manipulative frauds they are.

To begin with, the so-called "controversial" matters must exposed. Introducing a problem as controversial puts it in an unfavorable light at once. A pro-life bill is controversial, the decision to withdraw the methodological textbook on teaching human rights is controversial, the ban on peace parades is controversial, and so on. It is an obvious abuse of the Latin word "controversio" which means only that there are many opinions about the matter in question. But nowadays "controversial" is used to denote something not in keeping with liberal ideology, out of line with the rules of political correctness. Thus describing something as controversial is a method of stigmatizing it, and consequently it is not applied to matters and persons deemed politically correct, even though they may also be subject to different opinions and assessments.

This appropriation of certain terms, mainly of Latin origin, previously by the communist, now by the liberal ideology, is symptomatic of the media's manipulation.

When a matter can no longer be passed over in silence, or indeed suppressed, the media graciously raises the subject, routinely introducing it right away as controversial. What comes then? Different opinions are presented, some debaters point out pros, some cons. The first level of manipulation will be perceived only by those who count voices: how many were for and how many against, were they balanced, three each way, or let's say, five for, and one against? The problem is that in TV debates opinions follow one another very quickly and practically no viewer bothers to count. It is also crucial because this contributes to the general impression we get from watching. It influences what psychology defines as our subconscious. If we get the impression that the majority was for, then it must be the right cause, and so I am for it as well. Such a way of thinking is almost automatic for most viewers, and consequently this belongs to the standard repertoire of media manipulation.

On other occasions producers of a program are bent on simply confusing the viewers. It happens when a politically correct proposition is temporarily hard to promote. They orchestrate a hodgepodge of opinions in order to disorient people. In such situations the number of opinions for and against may even be balanced. However, the debate runs out of control, arguments are incompatible! Some debaters say that they are for because…, others that they are against because… Both opinions are substantiated, but… let's take an example. One debater declares that a textbook for teaching human rights must be rejected, because it promotes homosexuality and is anti-Christian; another counters that it has been accepted in forty countries. The latter argument does not answer the former. It would be an answer to the first debater's argument if the second debater claimed that the text was indeed Christian. The fact that so many countries accepted it, is no proof that it is a good textbook; it only proves that education is controlled in so many countries by left-wing liberals. And since we are a Catholic nation, we ought to keep our children as far away as possible from such a textbook, or rather a pseudo-textbook. Such a conclusion would be possible from an exchange of compatible arguments. However, in most media debates, we won't hear arguments answering one another. What we have, are simulated debates, with chaotic argumentation and no logic to them. Let us beware of such debates, their anchorpersons will not teach us logical thinking and any understanding of the world, they will not teach us responsibility or, for that matter, genuine... pluralism.

Successive Polish generations will let themselves be manipulated as long as the teaching of Latin and logic is not reintroduced in schools. These are the two subjects that form a cultured intellect. They were removed from the curriculum by communists, and the present-day Polish Republic has not reintroduced them during the fifteen years of its existence. Isn't it time that they were reintroduced by a Poland looking to the future? It would serve both the media people and politicians well, so that they begin to speak clearly, distinctly and with understanding most importantly using logic.

The Caricature

Muhammad's caricature published by numerous newspapers over the world precipitated an avalanche of reactions to which there seems to be no end. There have already been some fatalities, so far only among the protesting followers of Allah who were shot at by the military. However, the caricaturist cannot feel safe either, as government representatives of the states in which Islam is the official religion, set prizes not just for capturing the culprit, but for killing him forthwith. These rewards were considerable. They amounted to the sum of six million pounds. Imagine: for one small drawing, a few paltry lines...

The word "caricature" comes from the Latin "*carricare*" – "to load a cart". Therefrom, developed the Italian "*caricatura*" (literally: "loading"), used in the sense of overloading, overdoing something, or exaggerating. Exaggeration may sometimes be hilarious if it does not hurt anyone, but sometimes it may be nasty and dangerous when it is too aggressive. Just as an overloaded cart may break and collapse. Such was the case this time. The cart collapsed and spilled its load all over the world. Some people rashly attempted to involve Poland in the consequences. One cannot sometimes help but wonder why some journalists are so infantile, unless they are outright mercenaries, following the directives of some agencies (not only news agencies!), since one has to be pretty stupid to try to attack Islam.

A few paltry lines... But it must be stressed that religions, particularly monotheistic ones, are extremely sensitive to the iconosphere, more than to the word. Historically, it comes from the fact that an image appeals to everyone, and the word only to those who can read (and understand) and they were (and possibly still are) in the minority. A word is abstract, and an image concrete. Whatever the explanation, the fact is that in the history of the great monotheistic religions there were violent and sometimes bloody controversies over images, known as iconoclasm. They involved Judaism and Christianity (in Byzantium in the eighth century and during the Reformation), and occurred also within Islam. At the extreme, they resulted in the ban on any artistic presentations, in the destruction of sculptures and paintings, in the killing of people who defended them. Religious wars are to be feared.

Islam prohibits not only presentations of God, but of people and animals as well, not to mention Muhammad. This is an absolute prohibition. In art, only geometric and plant motifs are allowed. These are principles that have been observed for ages. They are religious principles. The entire domain of art is subject to the precepts of religion. There is no leeway of artistic freedom, of aesthetic considerations as such. All art is either religious, or antireligious. Anyone entering the realm of Arab civilization ought to know this.

Current Western luminaries are totally misguided by the Christian, and particularly Catholic tolerance, not so much in the matter of principle dogmas, but as to the freedom allowed artists in seeking inspiration and selecting subject matter for their art. In the Latin tradition, not everything is subject to religious criteria. The consequences of transgressing the domain of the sacred are also different. No one is executed by a firing squad for blasphemy. No prizes are set for killing a culprit. The assumption is that after so many centuries of dire experiences, people of the West got wiser and will not be duped by things like that anymore.

It is not so, however. Time and time again, we witness provocations of a blasphemous nature, perpetrated in the name of freedom, either personal or artistic. Both justifications are unreasonable, or bluntly speaking, stupid.

Freedom so construed, that is, freedom which does not respect the authentic rights of others – and such is the right of Christians to have their religion respected – contradicts itself, since it does not prevent an offending artist from being robbed, maimed or even killed at another's whim, in the name of freedom. If absolute freedom were the supreme right, everything would be permissible. War would be the only consequence of such a position.

When it comes to artistic freedom, there are indeed so many other subject matters and areas of experimentation that encroaching upon the sphere of religion is at best improper.

Religion ranks higher than art as it comes from God, while art is totally of man's making. How can art be placed higher than religion? Man above God? This notion must be dismissed in short order. It shows the supreme decline of culture! Total meanness! Complete divorce from reason!

So many artists have lost their bearings. Far too many. They squander their talent, or make up for its shortcomings by provocation and sensationalism. May this bitter experience of the caricatures make them realize that religion must not to be trifled with. It's not worth the trouble.

The Model Boy

Parents today more and more frequently expect the schools not only to educate their children, but also to raise them. Their explanation is simple: we don't have time, we work hard, and what's more, we don't know how to go about it, and the school has specialists. Indeed, scholarship has so advanced in many fields that it is hard to imagine parents acting as their children's teachers. Indeed, getting acquainted with educational theories is a full-time study as dozens of pertinent master's and doctor's theses, monographs and encyclopedias are being published all the time.

Still, normal people cannot help but rebel against such a proposition. They exclaim and question: Wait a minute, for thousands of years it was parents who took responsibility for bringing up their children, and now it should be totally given over to specialists? From kindergarten to university?

It is obvious that very few parents are as knowledgeable as university professors. One professor is not as knowledgeable as another. Specialization has ventured so far that even within one discipline scholars have a hard time not only agreeing on specific problems, but even communicating about them. So specialists must not be overestimated. Especially when it concerns the wellbeing of our children.

It must be remembered that educational theories are based on different concepts of human nature, derived from different philosophies, sometimes even ideologies. Further philosophies as well as ideologies vary widely. One philosophy says that human nature is not different from an animal's, another that a human being is like a machine. One ideology gives humans absolute freedom, another turns them into slaves.

When an educational theory is constructed on such premises, even if it is "scientifically" supported by so many authorities, scholars and many specialists with their distinctions, a normal person should shy away from it, especially a parent; be it a mother or a father, or both. They are rightly afraid for their child since specialists implementing such theories can really damage the child. In such matters one must be guided by common sense. It is not a hypothesis concerning the existence of water on Mars, about which scientists might reasonably argue. It is the matter of a child's very well-being, one special Chris or Mary, Bill or Kathy. In their case, their own parents will always remain the best specialists.

What is the gravest noticeable error of the educational theories currently predominating? It is an error looming over pedagogy for at least a hundred years, and whose consequences we witness every day, both in private and in public life. Stages of human life have been atomized, with a special idolization of childhood. Thus we have beautiful kids, but immature husbands, wives and parents. This pedagogical misconception was perceptively already pointed out decades ago by the great expert on ancient civilizations, Tadeusz Zieliński, who warned in his *Educational Ideal in Antiquity and in Our Time*, published in 1929: "Present day pedagogy too highly cherishes the idea of a model boy or girl; it should be replaced by the idea of a boy or girl who will mature into a model man or woman".

Precisely! We keep forgetting that a child must grow into an adult, and not just any adult, but an adult man or an adult woman, a responsible person, living up to the highest standards. One cannot remain a boy or a girl all their life, not even a model one. Unfortunately, this is what occurs more and more frequently. Educationalists seem to have forgotten that a human being must be looked at integrally, from the perspective of an entire lifespan, with particular stress on the smooth passage from one stage of life to the next, not on keeping them apart. Childhood may be adorable as such, but it is not to be idolized as life's goal. Maturity is the goal.

Today, the gender most at risk of remaining immature is the male, or should he be called "a boy" instead? We come across such boys in many families: grown-up men who don't know what it is to be a husband and father; we also encounter them in public life and in the world of politics. Among the essential characteristics of a boy-man is his having been pampered and spoiled, his thinking only about himself in the belief that he is entitled to everything, not feeling responsible for anybody and anything since others will take care of it for him, complaining to Momma about every little thing that displeases him. When he eventually gets married, he treats his wife as any odd woman, and his children as a burden since he has to secure a living for them, which he doesn't do too long, anyway. That's what today's boy-men are like, and when, God forbid, they become politicians, they will run to the media with their complaints and cry to the anchorwoman about how they have been slighted by other boys. This good lady will hold them and caress them, and berate the bad boys. There are more and more such man-boys, because their own sons, or real boys, emulate the big boys, or their Papas. So it turns into a vicious circle.

Parents should reflect on this if they care for the well-being of future generations, their own children included. Neither school, nor specialists will be a substitute for motherly love or for the wisdom and experience of one's own father. Being brought up by one's parents is a vital and indispensable element of reaching maturity. That's what parents must remember, and what children must have the right to expect from them. This is the age-old path to the correct development of a human being.

The Boyfriend

It was from the West that the trend has come for girls to have boyfriends, and so our fourteen-year olds have fiancés now. It's hard to say what they really understand by it, but the fact is that more and more young girls, not to say kids, play grown-ups. Their parents don't mind. They are proud that their daughter is popular, not different from the other girls and modern. She has a boyfriend, a few years older than her. He comes in his car to pick her up and they take a drive somewhere.

It is understandable that children are naïve, but that parents should be so unconcerned is staggering. Don't they realize that at such a tender age this is playing with fire? Who will suffer the consequences which aren't that difficult to anticipate? What will this or that escapade end with?

Bringing up a teenage girl is not an easy proposition nowadays. It was much easier in the past. Girls from good families were sent to finishing schools where they were prepared for the life of future wives and mothers, ladies of high religious and patriotic principles. Today even the surviving schools for girls are totally different, striving to be modern, with curricula conforming to the ministerial directives from above. They offer some amount of learning, but no education providing the means to form a human being according to the traditional model.

Finishing schools of old will not return. They were the product of a society of gentry and aristocracy that no longer exists. They would be a pretentious and ridiculous anachronism today, but some of that legacy should be preserved. Computer skills are modern, but the skill of graciously inviting and greeting guests, setting the table, polite conversation, creating a nice atmosphere, running the house in the traditional Polish style, all these are no small things, not outdated by any means. Unfortunately, many women aren't familiar with them anymore. They are modern: they pour boiling water on some soup mix and serve it with fast food for dinner. Then they wonder why their husbands and children don't want to stay home, and everything disintegrates. What's the use of a husband anyway?

A writer who succeeded in magnificently demonstrating what a girl should be like to preserve her youth and charm, was the twentieth-century Polish author Kornel Makuszyński. His novels also answer the question of how a girl should treat boys. Not as boyfriends, not as fiancés, but as companions. A teenage girl should meet many of them, maintain nice, friendly, funny relations with them, and that's all. This means that boys should also be raised in the same spirit by their parents, so that they know how to be companions and even gallant towards girls. Makuszyński knew what was going on in the colorful soul of a growing girl, even though he swore that it was an unfathomable secret.

Teenage years can be a beautiful period of youth, not childlike anymore, somewhat carefree still, but not yet quite like those of an adult. However this carefree attitude cannot extend into all spheres of adult life, or they will thwart it. Something may be lost, irretrievably. One might get burnt and pay with one's integrity. That is why I admire Makuszyński for having written novels that were avidly read by several generations of Poles, and that are still being appreciated by young readers whose elders know how to encourage them. As a child needs warmth, a young girl needs companionship and friendship, not a pretend betrothal. Everyone's life is future-oriented, but its progress should not be unduly precipitated.

Youth is an explosive time. It brings an explosion of biology on the one hand, and of sensitivity and spiritual quests on the other. The point is that it should result in an integral maturing of the young person. The force of biology ought not to be so much suppressed, but rather submitted to a sublimating and ennobling process. This is the secret of harmonious growth. When biology becomes the focus, it can poison the psyche, cripple the morale and hinder intellectual development. So it must be monitored, especially since today biological impulses are used as a devious method of enticing and depraving people, young people in particular, who, not suspecting danger, let themselves be molded, swim in droves with the tide, while reasoning that everybody does so, it is up-to-date and trendy. There is no other group so susceptible to mass manipulation as the young who believe, in fact, that they are original.

Education cannot be a mass process, as each person is a unique and original being. This is especially true of the education of a young girl who can so easily lose her charm if she turns into a woman too soon. Thus parents should watch their children carefully and protect their youth. This is a treasure that will pay off for the rest of their lives.

The Man in the Family

It is much easier to show a woman's role in the family today than a man's. The woman's role hasn't changed for ages except for the fact that women started to work professionally. So what has happened to the man? The man used to be the head of the family, but it is doubtful whether he is any longer. In Poland, twice as many women have a higher education, and in the fields of humanities masters' degree holders are predominantly women. So women are better educated than men not only statistically, but in reality. What is more, technical education is only specialized training for a profession, not a real, broad education. It does not expand cultural horizons, for culture has its basis in the humanities. Mastering the skill of building bridges or constructing airplanes does not teach the art of reading poetry, understanding Greek theatre and appreciating national history. A man won't typically sit with his child to help him or her do homework, study Polish or a foreign language, music, art or religion. He is more and more alienated from his closest family members. But he won't admit it. He runs away instead.

But where does he run to? If he is bright he'll search for self-realization in a professional career. He is convinced that what counts is his achievements, and the family is there to admire him. That's how intelligent men fall into the trap of pathological egocentrism, which isn't the same as egoism. The latter consists in doing everything for oneself or from one's perspective only, while egocentrism is the belief that one is the center of the universe and should be the object of admiration and adoration. A man so convinced will magnanimously take his child and wife biking once a month and will buy them ice cream. Since pursuing a career is time-consuming, he will seldom be home, and when he comes home he will be tired and oblivious. He will sit listlessly before the TV and jump from channel to channel, recovering from daylong stress. He has, after all the next day's work in front of him.

Less talented men concentrate on earning money. This commands the respect of family members because money is needed. The market abounds in offers, our eyes are greedy for things we don't have yet, or if we do, we'd like to have newer, better models. The prevalent way of spending time together is shopping. One can spend the better part of the day in mammoth supermarkets, walking from one rack to the next, sipping soft drinks and eating multicolored ice cream. When malls start including chapels, all of Sunday's activities will be centered there as well. However, it is the places in which we spend our time which contribute substantially to organizing our thoughts. How would one describe the thoughts of a person spending an inordinate amount of time in a world designed for the sole purpose of stimulating our desire to possess? Such a person does not think, but only reacts.

Men are in a difficult position today. They are a relic of the patriarchate, a burden they are unable to carry, because they are not being prepared for it. The idea of equality or partnership is fiction. When the man is not in charge, the woman is. There is no power-sharing in the way one's family is run, and no voting. Concrete matters are always closer to a woman's heart. A woman knows that a child must be fed, washed, dressed and sent to school. She also knows that on Sunday one must don one's best clothes and go to church. That after a day's work one must relax and have a good night's sleep. A woman does not get idly lost in thought.

But a man does. He lets his thoughts wander, pursues abstractions and chases ideals. If he is not a disciplined thinker, he will get lost among chimeras and start talking rubbish. He will most likely find his hobbyhorse in politics, and talk about it day in, day out. He doesn't share in the life of his family, takes less interest in his work, but he can talk politics all the time. He doesn't know when his children leave home or what his wife dreamt of when they tied the knot. Something is eating at him and he feels unfulfilled. So he embraces this new passion, invents scenarios, has a global vision of the history of mankind, illustrated by examples from newspaper and TV news. With his harangues he is estranged from his surroundings. Pathologically ambitious and conceited, he won't let himself be persuaded that he can blunder. He instead flexes his muscles and defies criticism.

Paradoxically, in great measure those who are responsible for all this are... women. This is so because they fail to bring up their sons to be men. Because they do not guide their interests, especially in the initial stage, toward the humanities. There will be enough time for a boy to study to be an engineer or a physician, but first each and every one of them must grow into a wise, responsible and sensitive human being, able to interpret what nation and what creed he belongs to, what principles he should abide by and what goals to aim at in life. A bridge spans two shores, but does not know which road to take. A surgeon will stitch a wound, but can't tell you what the secret of good health is.

Cornered, stripped of authority, accused of molestation or abuse, men have surrendered. They don't know how to be husbands and fathers. They seek refuge in their work, or tread in women's footsteps. It's a shame, since their wives and children need them. Not as geniuses, millionaires or workaholics, but as husbands and fathers.

Demoralization Is Ideology

The extent of demoralization, especially by the media, has reached such alarming proportions that it is hard to consider it accidental. Obscene pictures, vulgar language and perverts; it all adds up to a trend whose role can be compared only to the role of ideological indoctrination under communism. In fact, present-day pornography is even worse than communist indoctrination. As formerly no book, even a chemistry or physics textbook, could be approved for print unless it mentioned the teachings of Marx and Lenin, so today every tabloid, almost every magazine, not to mention TV programs and especially films, has to abound in things offending human dignity, breaking all canons of civility, morality and decency. This trend, pursued with obsessive persistence, is a well thought-out, intelligent and cunning program which could be devised only by evil incarnate. Consequently, almost each film includes pornographic scenes or scenes with perverts. Most glossy magazines run interviews with stars or psychologists discussing the ways of approaching a fifth marriage or a new partner or how to break all taboos in general. Similar questions are highlighted in song lyrics, frequently tinged with a touch of Satanism.

Demoralization harms children and teenagers the most since they are unconscious of what is hidden behind all this, and what price one has to pay later in life when they are lost and alone, having left behind compromised love and friendship. Parents are helpless or not fully aware of what's going on, or even worse, totally permissive, wanting to be modern, trendy, like everyone else.

Indeed, when people try to oppose demoralization, they are accused of being backward and not in keeping with the times. They will meet with derision, or with the charge that they are subverting democracy, blocking progress and assaulting freedom. When such arguments are put forward, it is evident that we are in the midst of an ideological war. We cannot help but conclude that demoralization and depravation, with pornography as their weapon, amounts to an ideology or is the tool of an ideology.

Which ideology is it? It isn't democracy, nor even liberalism. It is the old familiar socialism. Let us not forget that nineteenth-century socialism struck deep roots in the class of poor people who left villages and migrated to towns in search for work. They created enclaves of blue-collar workers, neither rural, nor urban. They were people becoming further and further divorced from familial and religious traditions. That is how the proletariat and communism were born, and revolutionary slogans began to be promulgated as a means of subverting the state and the Church. To a certain degree it succeeded. But as soon as the proletariat had played its role, its masses became not only unnecessary, but outright dangerous to the people who came to power. The proletariat had to be once more subjugated or even annihilated, as was the case in the Soviet Union.

Today the new proletariat is... the youth. Blue-collar workers have became part of the establishment. They often have better jobs and houses than many a white-collar worker and highfalutin' slogans don't impress them anymore. And the young? More and more of them are, in a way, homeless. Parents work long hours, and come back home too tired to pay much attention to their progeny. Don't they also need to have some rest, the right to watch a show on television, or the latest instalment of a soap opera? What's more, there are more and more divorced couples (it is becoming a veritable plague), so that children live with one parent only, and so become highly vulnerable, and frequent victims of a kind of mental mutilation. Our youth is homeless if we consider that merely four walls and a roof alone do not make a home, but that one is built on the interpersonal bond that ought to exist between parents and children, the bond of mutual love as well as responsibility.

This is what socialists, these engineers of the souls, utopians, communists, are waiting for. They want to captivate the souls of the young, their sensibilities, their confusion, their openness, and unfortunately, their naïveté. Because the young, in addition to their numerous wonderful virtues, their charm and their freshness, manifest one natural fault. They are naïve. They are inevitably naïve because they are inexperienced. They don't know how perfidious, callous and ruthless people tend to be, that there are whole groups devoid of any moral restraints who lurk waiting for victims wherever they can be found. As before, the deep but innocent hope to escape poverty was the bait that lured the proletariat, so today naïveté is what lets unscrupulous individuals attract and manipulate tin he young in all possible ways. The young can easily be taken in, especially since their parents are confused or indifferent, and politicians are totally absorbed by politics.

The young cannot defend themselves from demoralization on their own. Politicians alone cannot defend them, either. The main role in this belongs to the parents. If parents tolerate demoralization, they had better bear in mind that it is they who will be responsible for the corruption of their offspring. Conversely, if they understand their role, they can start the process of working out ways of protecting children that would engage politicians, teachers and clerics. Without the cooperation of parents it is virtually impossible to challenge and resist demoralization in any meaningful way.

The Marxist Stamp

The degree to which the humanities were paralyzed by Marxism in postwar Poland is unimaginable. Philosophy, history, literary and legal theory, sociology, psychology, political science – all these are disciplines which the Communists endeavored to bring under total control, both ideologically and personally. A specific mentality and a specific language were developed. Thousands, hundreds of thousands, millions of books, periodicals, manuals and guidebooks steeped in Marxism were published. They assaulted teenagers and adults, elementary school and college students, journalists and teachers, firefighters and policemen. Some were indoctrinated brutally, as soldiers and officers of the People's Army, whose minds were subjected to a thorough brainwashing, with a particular attention to pulling them away from faith and the Church. Others were offered subtle "scientific" training which had the same aim of alienating them from Catholicism and the Polish tradition.

To compare Marxism to acid rain is not enough. More appropriate would be a comparison with asbestos, which up to this day can be seen covering many a house in Poland and whose vapors keep poisoning people. Even though there are hardly any surviving Marxists today who openly admit their former adherence to Marxism, or acknowledge their own publications of the past, "*scripta manent*", what was once written remains. One can go to a library, check out pertinent material and read.

One of the fundamental components of Marxist theory was a peculiar brand of historicism consisting of the following elements: the humanization of the "ape" through work, incipient communism, class struggle, and the triumph of communism. "Scholars" of every category were supposed to either prove one of these theses, or substantiate them as already proven. Naturally, their publications could not be without quotations from and reference to, the work of the classical Marxism, such as Marx himself or his comrade Engels, and had to abound in

107

Marxist terms, such as "class struggle", "bourgeoisie", "Catholic reaction", and other similar terms. In different countries Marxism had its own local variety, whose highlights added to the credibility of the proposed analysis.

When it comes to Polish history, the Marxist interpretation was simple: a class struggle went on between the gentry and the peasantry, with the former being lords, and the latter victims of oppression; the Catholic Church being the ally of the gentry, and heretics being the defenders of peasants. The conclusion was self-evident: only the downfall of the gentry and the Church would liberate the peasants from oppression and bring social justice. To substantiate such a picture, an author had to dig up suitable "facts" and quotations which was not that difficult if one was an expert in researching source materials.

This was the key applied to the interpretation of Polish history in the publications of a certain Professor Janusz Tazbir. Were it not for his early articles from the 1950s, it might not be that easy to pinpoint the Marxist key, since with the change of ideological atmosphere, his language underwent some modifications and touch-ups, though not definitive ones. It may be the reason why even the more recent publications of this author are simply indigestible to many Poles interested in the history of their country. Marxism, if one ever believed in it, cannot be totally erased, because it leaves an indelible stamp on one's mentality and language. Tazbir simply imbibed Marx, and did it… in Russian. With peculiar over eagerness – one might refer to the original, that is the German, version, but to the Russian one? In his article "Echoes of the Sixteenth-Century Class Struggles in the Opinions of the Polish Gentry" (*Historical Review*, XLIII, 1952), Tazbir informs his readers that the quoted passage can be found in the Russian version of Marx's *Capital*, published in Moscow in 1949, on page 615. A telling gesture.

What is the quotation? A very interesting one. Marxists were always annoyed by the fact that the Church could not be conveniently fitted into the pattern of class struggle because the Church (Tazbir adds his comment: "now as always") knew how to shape "its hierarchy from the best minds of the nation, without paying any attention to class origin or wealth" (*op. cit.*, p. 16). Precisely. How did he deal with it then? Tazbir writes indignantly: "These men [meaning people of non-noble origin], for the price of an earthly career or of eternal salvation, served the interests of the enemy class, betraying those of the class they came from" (Ibid.). Here we have the essence of Marxist thinking in a nutshell: no wonder that the Polish peasants, instead of slaughtering landlords as it happened in countries torn by religious wars, remained Catholic, and the most talented among them even succeeded in Church careers. For a Marxist, this was inconceivable. A betrayal "in the name of eternal life".

From the above article we also learn that the so-called 1573 Confederation of Warsaw, guaranteeing freedom of faith to dissidents in Poland, unprecedented in war-torn sixteenth-century Europe, was motivated by "the common class interests" of the nobles of various denominations (p. 14). What subtlety of diction, what depth of thought! The subsequent publications of this author bring more such gems of intellect.

In addition to top it all off, it must be mentioned that until recently Professor Tazbir presided over the Central Committee for Conferring University Degrees. Years after the supposed fall of communism in Poland! No comment.

The Media Guillotine

The reaction of the Muslim world to a few words quoted by Pope Benedict XVI made us realize what a powerful and indeed frightening force the media is. In a second, they can muster tens if not hundreds of millions of people to behave in a certain way. It makes no difference whether the speaker is quoting somebody else, that these are not his words. One can be guillotined by the media for a quotation. In fact, for any word if they so decree. Is this not sheer madness?

In this context, we should remember how unique European culture is. The culture assaulted by almost everyone nowadays. The culture hardly anybody wants to subscribe to anymore. Distancing themselves from it in the name of pluralism, in the name of openness, in the name of tolerance. Even though it was in this culture that democracy, freedom of speech and the right to search for truth were born. A priceless treasure. Other civilizations don't allow such things, they never did and probably never will. They may pretend, but they don't understand it and they don't have such needs.

When not only demonstrations arise in response to one centuries-old quotation, but also arson and killing, we cannot believe what we are witnessing. It isn't our world. It is a totally alien world. A different civilization. A gulf separates us from it. It is a world cut off from the world, a world alien to the exchange of thoughts, ideas and opinions.

Let us simply open a twenty-five-hundred-year-old work, one of the most difficult ones, i.e. Aristotle's *Metaphysics*. It begins not with what the author thinks, but what others thought. What Heraclitus thought, what Pythagoras thought and what Plato thought and why. Only after these accounts follow endeavors to disprove their theses. Not ruthlessly or unceremoniously, but by showing that their arguments are weak and that they do not hold when faced with the facts. What a magnificent lesson of humility and courage it was! The humility of listening to others and the courage of opposing them if they are wrong. Not opposing them by sheer force, but by the strength of reasoned argument.

Next let us open the *Summa Theologica* of St. Thomas Aquinas, which discusses the difficulties inherent in interpreting the Scriptures. It begins with interrogative sentences, such as: "Is God's existence a certainty?" Before we learn what St. Thomas thinks, we listen to various opinions, many of them those of recognized authorities of the earlier centuries. Then, after we have heard Thomas's proposition, we learn various objections to it, and finally a refutation of them. Having read it, we can come to our own rational conclusions as we have understood the different opinions and various arguments, and so we can come to a more thorough understanding of the problem.

This is how our common sense Western and European liberty was developed; it was allowed even when religion was the subject of controversy. Man has the right to ask questions, to ponder, to learn what others think, or thought. This is our European tradition in which we feel at home. We don't even allow it to be otherwise. Quoting somebody's opinion, even an utterly absurd one, is the norm of Western-style discussion. It was Socrates, then Plato, and afterwards Aristotle, and later St. Thomas Aquinas who, with pedagogical goodwill, listened to the most preposterous opinions, and quoted them before analyzing them scrupulously in order to correct them with surgical calm. Not by way of proclaiming anathema, but by showing where their errors might lie. This is our culture of discussion and searching for the truth. Someone's being in error and straying is no reason to hate them. They may even remain friends, as decreed in Aristotle's famous maxim: "*Amicus Plato, sed magis amica veritas*",which means, "Plato may remain a friend, even though truth is a greater one". Out of the same culture came the equally illuminating observation of the fifteenth-century Polish scholar and writer, Paweł Włodkowic: "*fides ex necessitate esse non debet*"; that is, "faith cannot be arrived at under duress". We understand this, it is obvious for us Westerners. So obvious that we condone even overt intolerance towards Christianity in the West itself. Without Christianity, there would be no Voltaire, that intelligent freethinker and mocker. Which culture, which religion would allow such mockery? None, besides Christianity.

The media assault on Pope Benedict XVI should dampen somewhat the zeal of European scribes who see all evil in Christianity. Were it not for Christian culture, with its roots in the tradition of Greek and Roman cultures, many of them would be illiterate or semiliterate, and wouldn't have the faintest idea about freedom or truth. Perhaps what happened will teach them a lesson, alerting them to the incalculable impact of the media on millions of people, which may push them towards good and evil equally.

There would be no harm, either, in at least some of these scribes broadening their familiarity with the tradition by reading Plato, Aristotle and St. Thomas Aquinas. It might help them revise their values and to come to respect ours.

The Freedom of a Child and Parental Authority

Assaults on the family continue. Amongst the many arguments aiming to destroy the family is that parents limit a child's freedom. While this is a ridiculous accusation let us nevertheless analyze it further.

But what is freedom? It is self-determination; we say that someone is free because they can determine their own fate. Making decisions is the nodal point of self-determination. Essentially everything depends on the ability to make the right decision. Anyone with some life experience realizes that making a decision, and the right decision at that, is no easy matter. It is dependent on one's presence of mind, integrity and ability to control one's emotions, and, finally, on experience. A person must, after all, suffer through a few bad experiences in order not to make hasty decisions.

Thus, if we think of a child's freedom not as mere whim or absence of limits but as the capacity for self-determination, i.e. as the ability to make the right decisions, then we will reach the conclusion that has a long way to go towards such an ability. It takes many years for the child to learn this ability and in order to do so it requires the right upbringing.

The role of the parents in the process of upbringing is indispensable because parents and children know each other better than anyone else. What binds them together is common blood, the home and tradition. While a teacher and a priest are also necessary, since the parents are not experts in every realm, nevertheless, the major initiative is always the parents' prerogative. Before a child is mature enough to comprehend and before it acquires the necessary experience she or he must live, and while living she or he must make choices. Who else is the child to ask if not the parents? They are, after all, the child's closest authority figures. This is normal and our Polish tradition also teaches this.

If someone attempts to oppose the child's freedom to parental authority then it is either the work of someone irresponsible or simply that of a thief attempting to steal the parents' child. This is no exaggeration. It turns out that there are plenty of thieves lying in wait for our children. The Nazi German state was such a thief and so was the socialist state. Both states stole children almost immediately after they were born.

But the ideologues of the new paradise on Earth are also thieves. They steal children in the name of a falsely-understood "freedom" and wreak havoc in the home. They also call self-destruction self-determination. Facts from everyday life, such as young boys high on drugs and lying on the street or girls prostituting themselves and waiting for an "opportunity" on one of the major roads, confirm this. This is no longer freedom. It is decadence.

It is important to remember that parents must inspire a royal, not a despotic authority in their children. It is love and wisdom that should speak through them, not egoism and short-sightedness. This means that parents too must learn how to be authority figures for their child since only then will their offspring grow into someone capable of self-determination. The child naturally trusts the parents and looks to them for acceptance and approval and the parents must not fail the child in this respect. More than two thousand years ago one of the ancient authors, a Pseudo-Aristotle, claimed that a man begins to fear someone toward whom he acts in a hateful and hostile way because he sees in him a tyrant. However, a true authority figure is someone whom a man admittedly fears but towards whom he also acts in a respectful and humble manner. The latter characterizes a good son's relationship with his father. Unfortunately, modern-day opponents of the family know only tyranny. What they don't know is the meaning of true authority and the way a human being earns the respect she or he deserves.

"An Enemy to Man and God"

Everyone is familiar with the name "Cyclops" though, perhaps, not everyone recalls that Odysseus and his companions visited the land of the Cyclopes on their voyage from Troy to their native Ithaca. A Cyclops was a monster that Homer described as follows in his *Odyssey*: "He is a boor that acknowledges no laws above himself (...), an enemy to man and God, and moreover does not have a pair of eyes like a man, but only one". Odysseus almost paid with his life for his visit at the Cyclops' cave. Only because of a trick was he able to save himself.

It is difficult to believe that one would be able to find an appropriate modern-day analogy for this fictional poetic tale written almost three thousand years ago. However, such an analogy actually exists, though it concerns not a handful of shipwrecked sailors but every person throughout the world.

Let us take a closer look. There is a minotaur Cyclops in almost every residence, usually located in a central place within the home. This is a television set. Americans even refer to it as the "one-eyed bandit" that mercilessly terrorizes everybody, both the residents and guests. It hypnotizes everyone with its one eye and pulls them into its cave from which it is very difficult to escape.

Many people will probably respond as follows: "This is an exaggeration. We don't sit in front of the TV for days on end and we also think for ourselves and we know how to watch television with the necessary critical attitude". Homer would, however, respond as follows: "I wanted to meet him and be invited as a guest./ It would have been better for me to never have met the cursed one at all".

A TV program is most often a montage. First, different fragments are recorded on tape and then they are edited, cut and reassembled. Only after this work is completed do millions of viewers actually see the broadcast. The montage is no mere

115

hand-sewing, the effects of which can be seen from far way, but a detailed computerized operation undetected by the naked eye. A program can be edited in such a way that everything will be contrary to reality: thieves can be policemen, the most serious person will laugh and the most important character will actually be one to whom no one paid any attention. The edited and reassembled events are like a sick man under anesthesia. Just as such a patient can undergo a serious operation and have a transplant of the most vital organs so too the meaning and order of events can be reversed. Critical viewing will be of no avail here for millions of people will be misinformed without even realizing it.

If only ten people witnessed an event then 100 million people all over the world will watch a program dedicated to it thanks to television. And if the TV program happens to be a biased one then how will all those people who were not eyewitnesses find out that they have just been the victims of media manipulation? Given the *embarrassment* of events, programs and information there are no realistic chances of controlling what and how the TV networks present issues.

Most TV viewers passively absorb images and rarely understand what they are really watching, who prepared it and for what purpose. It is as a result of television that our imagination, our thoughts and our feelings cease to exist in a well-ordered psyche. We can see this clearly by looking at the behavior of the young generation which has been brought up on television. Its attitude is characterized by aggressive reactions, lack of culture, inability to concentrate and the lack of respect for others and even their own parents. The TV mix is a very dangerous drink. It must truly be "an enemy to man and God".

But this is not all. In 1957 James Vicary presented his invention, called the tachistoscope, in the United States. Lawyers, observers and journalists were shocked. *Newsday* wrote: "This is the most alarming invention since the time of the atom bomb". *The New Yorker* agreed: "We have reached a sad age when one can break and enter into not only our homes but our minds as well". One of the editors of the *New York Journal –*

American concluded: "I am terrified that I will be pushed to act without knowing about it (...). I can also imagine an invisible commercial inclining me towards immorality".

Whence all this horror? The tachistoscope – this new atom bomb that was supposed to destroy not the body but consciousness – was simply a film projector that, using incredible speed (1/3,000 of a second), displays an image on the screen every five seconds. Of course the speed of the flash made it impossible for anyone to realize that something like this was taking place. Thus, one could be attentively watching an animal show, a melodrama or a detective show without realizing that a given image appears every five seconds for 1/3,000 of a second and affects the viewer's subconscious. What are the effects? When a tachistoscope was experimentally used at an American movie theatre and the image displayed was the inscription "Are you hungry? Have some popcorn" then popcorn sales increased by 50 percent over a six-week time.

In 1962 the tachistoscope was officially patented in the United States. Though in time attempts were made to ban the use of this atomic bomb, they never received the force of law. What are the results?

Let us imagine competition on the market for profits in the range of millions if not billions of dollars. We know of those one to three second cuts during a commercial. Perhaps they include short 1/3,000 second-long flashes? Or let us imagine an election campaign where the stakes are the taking of power in a country or altering attitudes towards a criminal system that lasted for fifty years in such a state... When watching TV we have no idea when we are dealing with a tachistoscope. But we do know that American technology is being widely employed in Poland and the techniques for affecting the subconscious have also undoubtedly made progress. It is scary to even contemplate.

There is much talk these days about human rights, including the right to privacy. But our subconscious is the most private and delicate part of us. Regardless of all the theories attempting to define what exactly the subconscious is, we do know that there is a high probability that the subconscious affects our conscious opinions and decisions. In order to make these as responsible, i.e. thought out, free and objective decisions, man must be shielded from influences of which he is not aware and which were specifically devised by individuals treating other people as objects of financial or political exploitation. Thus, so-called democracy, when confronted by the realities of this subconscious control, turns out to be a mere illusion and, what is more, the greatest of known dangers to date for the man of the late twentieth and early twenty-first century. So what should we do? How are we to defend ourselves?

Let us return to Homer. What did Odysseus do to save his own life and at least some of his companions? He got the Cyclops drunk on wine and, using a heated timber, burned his eye out so that the blinded monster could search for food only by groping around. We do not have to be so cruel. After all, TV waves only look for their victims by groping around. Let us then turn off our television sets or, better yet, get rid of them altogether. Why tempt the devil?

Rule by Technocrats

Albert Speer was one of the most important men behind the power of the Third Reich. Initially, he was Hitler's court architect. He quickly understood the scope of the Hitler's ideas and worked on both the staging of great political spectacles and the reconstruction of Berlin as the world's new capital. Later he even became the Minister of War. At Nuremberg he was sentenced to twelve years in prison.

Speer exemplified a man of tremendous intelligence who was called a genius of organization. However, his case also allows us the see the degree to which talent and intelligence can be devoid of any sense of moral responsibility. It is not difficult to understand how the uneducated masses, susceptible to propaganda and manipulation, become enchanted by some ideology, or system of perpetrating evil. But why can't intelligent, sometimes even very intelligent people, employ their intelligence to understand morality? Why do they cease to comprehend what is a truly good and what is actually evil? Why do their minds, in spite of their intelligence, also succumb to this moral torpor? Such questions come to mind when we hear people nowadays claim that the state must be a law-governed state and that the people in charge of government must be effective. Do we really mean any kind of law and any kind of effectiveness here? Is evil law truly law? Is effectiveness in doing evil truly effectiveness? Or perhaps evil law is simply violence and effective evil-doing is simply destruction. Sometimes a spade must be called a spade.

During the Nuremberg Trials, as the representative of a defeated empire, Speer had more time for reflection. It was then that he made a very accurate observation that has not lost its relevance even today. He pointed out the difference between older despotisms and modern totalitarianism. In his *Memoirs* he wrote: "But in this fatal epoch, besides human villainy, for the first time in history there appeared a factor that differentiated this despotism from all previous models and which will gain importance in the future. As the most important representative of technocracy [Speer was referring to himself], which thoughtlessly and without any restraints engaged all of its resources against humanity, I tried to not only admit but to also understand what happened. As my last word I said: Hitler's dictatorship was the first dictatorship of an industrial state during the modern technological era".[9]

Modern technology is the most dangerous of weapons not in the hands of madmen but of technocrats. The madman acts impulsively, under the influence of emotions and with a short-term goal while a technocrat is an intelligent person who acts with far-reaching long-term goals in mind. The problem is that the power of technology seems to possess some sort of magical property of dulling the moral senses. Technocrats, that are the people for whom technique is the main tool of action, begin to deify the tool itself to such a degree that their conscience becomes completely blind. It may take many a catastrophe for at least some of the technocrats to wake up and at least temporarily listen to their own conscience. But who will repair the evil already perpetrated?

It is worth quoting Aristotle's classic text: "Just as a well-developed man is the foremost of creatures so he is the worst of all if he breaks away from law and justice". The law of which Aristotle spoke was, first of all, rooted in God's law and natural law, which forms the basis of justice and a healthy conscience. "For the worst thing is armed iniquity and man is born equipped with a weapons which are mental and moral abilities which can be improperly used like no other. Therefore man without moral sensibility is the most wicked and savage of creatures..." (Aristotle, *Politics*, I, 12). Thus, it is not one's intellectual abilities that make a man great. On the contrary, such abilities can become the source of man's descent into barbarism so that he will become worse than an animal. This happens when he begins to lose his conscience and ceases to discern objective good from evil. Afterwards he devotes all the power

---

9. A. Speer, *Memoirs*, Warsaw 1973, p. 723.

of his intellect to destruction. Today technology is a mighty multiplication of intellectual power. An insane man who injures people with a knife or a wartime trick whereby the cavalry overruns the infantry is one thing. Using the weapons of mass destruction is another. If the usage of technology is devoid of moral restraints then, as a tool of evil, it is classifiable even as a crime against humanity.

Nowadays we ought to fear technocrats more than madmen. They are armed not only with military technology but also with administrative, financial, legal, journalistic and educational instruments. Because of this they can destroy and enslave millions of people throughout the world. Enchanted by its effectiveness they forget about man and the fact that he is a person, not a Guinea Pig to be experimented upon

These days raising people to be people is of the utmost importance. They become human beings not because of a high level of intelligence but primarily through a properly-shaped conscience. We must ensure that the young develop a sensitive conscience so that as adults they will use their intelligence, talent and technology only to do good and never to perpetrate evil.

Descartes and... Television

Today we are spoiled to the point where we search only for what is easy and pleasant. We are like old children. An adult, however, should not fear difficulty, including the difficulty of serious thought. Thanks to this he conditions himself to become wiser and wisdom is not at all easy.

While searching for the answer to why people watch TV so readily and why they are so quick to believe everything television tells them we must probe into the history of philosophy, to the days before TV was invented.

The famous René Descartes lived during the first half of the seventeenth century (1596 – 1650). He can be classified as one of the most important thinkers who had a powerful impact not only on philosophy but also on our Western culture.

How did this Cartesian position change our orientation? It changed our perception of human acts of cognition and love and of the sensory and spiritual orders. Real things were replaced by ideas. Descartes claimed that we do not know and love things as they are in reality but only the representations of those things existing in our conscience.

How is one to save the truth then if reality is unknowable? Both during the ancient and Medieval eras, despite the fact that different and often strange views were voiced, the classical definition of truth was the common heritage of the West: "*Veritas est adequatio rei et intellectus*". In other words, the truth is the agreement of cognition with reality.

For something to be true one must reconcile one's cognition, as expressed by a judgment, with the reality to which this judgment pertains. Thus, if I say that "John Smith is a tailor" and John Smith is really a tailor then my statement is true. If I also say that the mentioned John Smith exists and he really does exist then I am also speaking the truth. But if John Smith is actually a driver and says that he is a tailor then I am not telling the truth. These examples illustrating the classical definition of truth may seem banal, but only at first glance.

If, on the other hand, we follow Descartes then it turns out that we have no way of ascertaining what is true and what is false because all we can know are ideas. We have no way of contrasting that which we come to know and that which we speak of with reality because we cannot know reality itself.

Thus it is here that Descartes proceeds to perform a feat of intellectual acrobatics for he claims that while we do not come to know reality there are some ideas that must be true. These are *clear* and *well-defined* ideas. Thus, the criterion of deeming an idea to be true, i.e. compatible with reality, is their clarity and their well-defined nature, not authentic compatibility with reality. Moreover, a good God that would not wish to lead us into error was to be the guarantor of truth.

Philosophers eagerly accepted Descartes' theory that we come to know ideas, not reality, though they approached his notion of a divine guarantee with a large dose of skepticism, treating it as wishful thinking, having nothing in common with philosophy. Thanks to Descartes early modern and modern philosophy became divorced from reality thereby opening the field to ideology and speculation

Philosophers are aware of this but do people with an average education realize this? Unfortunately they do not. This is why they are susceptible to all kinds of ideological manipulation. But it is the mass audience, not the specialists that are the greatest victims. It turns out that TV gains credibility precisely by applying the Cartesian criterion of truth in its programming. The suggestion that an image on TV is true is based mainly on its *clarity* and *definition*. When compared with bland everyday life the world of television looks much more lively, colorful and "real". Anyone who ever visited a television studio was shocked by the number of powerful lights falling on the program participants form different directions. The point of all of this is to achieve the best possible image quality. Amateur films, made using home video cameras, are usually unlit or insufficiently lit and the image is therefore dark, flat and blurry. Even if one part of the image is bright the other might be dark. What ensues is a visual disorder which makes the viewing of home videos a boring and tiring task. Professionally-made movies however have the necessary clarity and definition because this makes them more attractive and even credible.

Often, when spending time with friends or family, we have a hard time concentrating on the topic of discussion or on ourselves if the TV is on. Our eyes tend to unwittingly drift towards the screen. People on TV are so well lit and so well-defined in terms of color and shape that they are much more of a stimulus to the human eye than real people. However, the people around us – mothers, fathers, grandparents, children, neighbors – are real people, not TV images. In order to verify if the images actually correspond to reality we would have to enter the studio and take a look at all the lights, cameras and decorations imitating a room or a salon. Even though there are real people in that room a million viewers will not be able to enter because the crowd won't fit in the room. An outsider won't be allowed in either if he doesn't have a pass. The viewer who is completely enchanted by the image will therefore be completely detached from reality. The clarity and definition which he seems to accept as the criterion of truth is not generated by reality but by lights which he does not see.

All of this is important to remember before we turn on the TV in search of truth, and before we claim that something must be true because we can see it with our own eyes... on TV. Eyes glued to the television set are not good witnesses.

Christian Humanism
and the Challenges of Modern Culture
in Post-Communist States

Post-communism is one of the most difficult phenomena to define. It pertains to countries of the Soviet Bloc in which communism was the official ideology. But communism could have a different character, from a very aggressive to a relatively mild one, in every Soviet Bloc state. Communist regimes were particularly negatively predisposed towards religion and private property. The status of Christianity in the communist states was diverse and ranged from complete atheism, as in the Soviet Union or East Germany, to the unquestionable social and even political force of the Catholic Church in Poland.

It was in the Soviet Union during the years 1918 – 1939 that one-hundred-thirty bishops and 200,000 priests were murdered, 300,000 priests imprisoned and 40,000 churches blown up. Meanwhile, after the introduction of communism in Poland after World War II, in spite of the initial heavy-handed persecution, show trials (one thousand clergymen were arrested, out of which eighty were murdered) and even the imprisonment of the Primate (Stefan Cardinal Wyszyński), the Church managed to defend itself. The rising number of vocations to the priesthood, mass participation in Church services and the construction of new churches was testimony of this. Some bishops-ordinaries were able to build several hundred churches (as many as three hundred!) in their diocesies, in spite of the government and with great popular involvement. Then, finally, during the days of deep communism Poland gave the world a Pope. In every communist country save Poland private ownership of land was abolished. There were, of course, some collective farms in the Polish People's Republic but a significant portion of the land remained in private peasant hands.

The end of the Cold War and the disintegration of the Soviet Bloc allowed many countries to regain their independence, including both countries that had, as republics, integral parts of the Soviet Union (e.g. Lithuania, Latvia, Estonia) as well as satellite states (e.g. Poland, Bulgaria, Romania). Those countries changed their systems from communism to capitalism, from socialism to liberalism. However, this is a strange system and a bizarre situation which signifies the word "post-communism" but does not explain it. It was, after all, the communists themselves that became the main beneficiaries of this and were not held accountable for all the evil they brought upon their societies over the decades. They eagerly divided up state property amongst themselves.

Property is no longer subject to a communist system but much of it is nevertheless in the hands of communists. Post-communism is the takeover of state property by communists. They took over land, factories, the media (including TV networks) and schools. But have the communists given up their ideological goals? Is neo-Marxism, which so easily comes to terms with liberalism on the ideological plane, perhaps not an element of post-communism?

When the Soviet Bloc fell apart the states that composed it opened up to the West. But what was the first to arrive from the West? Where atheism reigned sects checked in while in countries with a living Church a process of intensive secularization began. On the ideological plane this invasion was sponsored by liberalism and post-modernism. The former preached moral permissivism and anti-clericalism while the second was the destruction of realistic cognition and the traditions of Western culture. Societies that were morally and intellectually weakened by communism began to totter. They were not prepared for these new threats whose success rested more on the weakness of the victims rather than their own strength.

Let us remember that for decades the West appeared as a dreamed-of liberator in the minds of communist-ruled societies. But the "West" that actually made its way into the media, the Church and the universities was strangely suspect. One could sometimes be under the impression that its ends were the same as the goals of the communists although the means were different, i.e. more "democratic". As far as abortion, euthanasia, anti-clericalism and demoralization went the West was no different from the East. It became increasingly apparent that any struggle for authentic human rights must be waged by Christian humanism. But what is Christian humanism?

There are three humanisms. The word "humanism", though it is derived from the Latin *humanus* (man), is actually a modern neologism (F.J. Niethammer, 1808). It means the orienting of civilization toward man as the center of the realms of culture. Throughout the history of humanism different currents, including Christian humanism, can be identified. This one is a relatively late arrival. It appeared in response to Renaissance humanism, which was a pagan rebirth the West, and socialist humanism, which was atheism.

During the ideological struggle with Christianity, already during the Reformation period, the trend emerged to oppose humanism, whose main object of interest was man, to the theocentric Middle Ages which, it was claimed, neglected human affairs in favor of abstract scholastic speculation. Renaissance humanism was not originally atheistic. It did not deify man but invoked a whole pantheon of pagan, Greek, Roman and Oriental gods. The deification of man appears only in nineteenth-century socialism which posited the alternative that man and God were incompatible. Thus, the concept of Christian humanism was introduced to stem the tide of neopaganism and socialism which turned out to be merely pseudo-humanisms. Moreover, Christian humanism emphasizes that Christianity is not detached from man because it is man that is the subject of culture. But because man is neither his own creator nor an end unto himself, since God serves as both, then humanism can only be Christian. It must be Christian because God is neither Zeus nor Zarathustra but One God of the Trinity.

The official culture of our day, i.e. the culture that is promoted by the mass media, legalized by governments and taught at universities, is burdened by the double heritage of false humanism, i.e. pagan and socialist humanism. There is no room for Christian humanism however.

Without understanding communism it is impossible to understand post-communism. The system obtaining in Soviet Bloc countries was known as "real socialism". The status of property was an issue of utmost importance: communism negates private property while liberalism is based on it. In the complex communist ideology, nationalisation (i.e. state takeover of property) was not an end in itself. The goal was to deprive society of the so-called base which would allow it to cultivate tradition and develop its own culture independently of the state. Communism's objective was to destroy personalist culture in favor of mass culture. Man was to be reduced to an element of society; he was nothing outside of society. If being a person means the possession of certain human rights guaranteed by the state and civilization then, under communism, man was deprived of these both from the point of view of instituted law and from the means towards their realization. Authentic human rights are expressed in natural law. Private property, which St. Thomas Aquinas referred to as a complement to natural law, was a means of securing them.

Under communism the right to life did not extend to conception and unborn persons. A married couple could obtain a divorce. Lying was the *modus operandi* of the media and government. It is a paradox that natural law is violated in the name of "human rights" in the West also. After all, neither unborn life, nor marriage are protected. In fact, homosexual marriages are being legalized, which is something that even communist regimes dared not do.

With the exception of the attitude towards private property, one can get the impression that today the Western and Eastern socialists have converged and form one family. Europe is losing its Western identity and its Christian heritage. But where is the Christian intelligentsia in all of this?

A Christian intelligentsia does not fall from the sky but is, instead, the product of a long process of development. This process begins at the home and leads through the Church and the schools. At home parents have less and less time for their children. There is no time for conversation and discussion, nor for proper education and upbringing. It is the TV and the street that is raising the children. But television cannot bring up an elite, but merely a dull uniform man that is incapable of reflection, crushed under the sheer chaos of information and irritated by his own primitive reactions. The words of Heraclitus apply to such people very well: the eyes of men who have the souls of barbarians are bad witnesses.

Meanwhile, the schools are undergoing constantly new reforms and experiments whose patron and inspiration is John Dewey, a bitter enemy of Christianity. In Catholic schools only the religion is still Catholic. But even this was changed to the sociology of religion, or so-called religious studies, which sometimes happens to be taught by people of other faiths or even atheists. They can teach it because religious studies, which presents different religious cults, including idolatry and animism, is not the same thing as religion, which opens man up to the true God and Transcendence. Will a young man remain a Christian if an atheist teaches him religious studies at school? Especially when the teacher presents the subject matter with a large dose of skepticism if not outright contempt and hatred. It is very doubtful.

A Catholic education was based on the *trivium*, which was the basis of a humanist education. What followed was the *quadrivium*. The crowning of the *septem artes liberales* was philosophy. After World War II, when the communists began to implement their reforms of the education system, they intentionally removed rhetoric, logic and philosophy from high school curricula. Greek was also eradicated while Latin was also eventually phased out. Thus were destroyed the foundations of a classical, i.e. a humanistic education which granted the ability to understand diverse texts and to verbalize thoughts. The *trivium* was replaced by the *quadrivium*, i.e. the mathematical subjects, and the natural sciences (biology, chemistry, physics). It was now possible to start producing the new generation and the socialist mass man. Ideology was to become his wisdom. This ideology was pushed everywhere, at every level of schooling, but it was to permeate the minds of the intelligentsia, i.e. university students. Thus, every student was required to pass an exam on Marxism.

In order to break the clerics they were recruited into the army. When the communists created the Fourth Department of the Ministry of the Interior in Poland (i.e. the secret police) every cleric had a file dedicated to him in which the secret police gathered all sorts of information that could be useful for the purpose of blackmail or recruitment. Communism was a system of intelligently-organized evil. Are Westerners sure that it is over, since in many post-communist countries communists are in charge and not all countries underwent the process of vetting (*lustracja*)? Do they realize whom they are so easily accepting into the European community? Are they not being rather bit naïve?

In order to stem the tide of this evil what was necessary was morality growing out of tradition and strengthened by religion. In order to decipher this evil an educated mind was necessary. Marxists feared traditional morality. In order to combat it they promoted "socialist morality" and also formed silent alliances with so-called progressive Catholics. Thus, traditional Polish morality, which grew out of Christianity, was outflanked.

On the other hand, the Marxists also understood that philosophy posed a threat to their ideology. But not all philosophy. Just as some controlled political pluralism was permitted in the form of a pro-regime peasant party (ZSL: the United Peasant Party) and a liberal party (SD: Democratic Party) so too phenomenology and analytical philosophy was taught at some state universities. Not only did they pose no threat to Marxism but some Marxists, looking to raise their prestige as philosophers, piggy-backed off of phenomenology or analytical philosophy. They also invoked positivism and neo-positivism. But not out of the love of truth but because the conception of science worked out within their framework was very anti-theological and anti-metaphysical.

The real enemy of Marxism, both ideologically and philosophically, was Thomism. It was the enemy of Marxism

130

ideological because it was tied to Christianity and the Catholic Church and it was a philosophical enemy because only Thomism represented realism. Marxism did not fear phenomenology or analytical philosophy because they were, like Marxism, brands of idealism. The starting points of phenomenology are phenomena arrived at after employing *EPOCHÉ*, i.e. the detachment of content from existence. Analytical philosophy's starting point is language at the level of the senses. But if existence is the *reason of being* then neither phenomenology nor analytical philosophy can be classified as realistic philosophy. Marxism is also not realistic because it reduces being to matter and matter to impressions.

One major Marxist in Poland, as well as a member of the Central Committee of the Polish United Workers' Party (i.e. the Communist Party), wrote the following about Thomism: "The condition for a complete ideological victory of the Marxist-Leninist worldview in Poland is, i.a. overcoming the ideological influences of philosophical currents that are alien in class terms. Of primary importance here is Thomist philosophy, a philosophy that is clearly fideistic in nature, and one that is the official philosophy of Catholic schools".[10]

Though it ultimately proved impossible to halt the development of classical philosophy in Poland, we do not know what the future holds. Modern-day socialism is shifting its main emphasis from ideology to technology. The latter has its own hidden ideology and philosophy though they are not as aggressive as Marxism which wanted to replace not only philosophy but also religion.

Marxism required its own philosophy because it had to come in conflict with an educated stratum in society. Initially, pre-war non-communist professors were allowed to hold some professorships, though not out of respect for them as scholars,

---

10. A. Schaff, *Narodziny i rozwój filozofii marksistowskiej* [*The Birth and Development of Marxist Philosophy*], Warsaw 1950. See: M. A. Krąpiec, *Byt i istota* [*Being and Essence*], Lublin 1994. It is interesting to note that Schaff includes the number of books by Marxist authors printed by 1950: *Selected Works* by Marx and Engels, 200,000; Lenin's *Materialism and Empiriocriticism*, 275,000; Stalin's *On Dialectical and Historical Materialism*, 300,000 plus. Catholic publishing institutions were of course hamstrung by government limitations such as censorship and insufficient paper allotments (in a centrally-planned socialist system paper was rationed).

but in order to allow young Marxists to educate themselves. When they obtained the necessary degrees they replaced the old professors and began to implement the top-down ideologization of the humanities.

This Marxist threat to the humanities had at once an ideological, personal, administrative and financial character. But the greatest paradox came about when within Christian circles an inferiority complex *vis-à-vis* Marxist humanities and related currents appeared. The new regime created intellectuals salons in a truly Byzantine style. For some scholars gaining access to these salons proved to be an irresistible dream. It is the same way nowadays.

The treasure of classical philosophy is based not only on its realism but also on its theoretical character. Marxism recognized only practical goals. But these were not goals as understood in the realist sense of complementing and improving nature but, often, in a very aprioristic way. Let us recall that a goal, according to Aristotle, is actualized in a natural form. If, however, the goal is outside of nature, or contrary to nature then, on the political and cultural plane, it leads to totalitarianism. This is because totalitarianism does not take account of nature-subject. This was what ultimately established the totalitarian nature of communism, since it was pragmatism with idealistic ends in the name of which one could completely ignore reality.

The totalitarian nature of Marxist communism in its Soviet version was visible to Catholic intellectuals raised on classical philosophy. The Western intelligentsia, increasingly more diluted by liberalism, lacked this clarity of vision. It saw the evil of communism, but for political, not intellectual reasons. The Western intelligentsia, journalists and academics leaned to the Left.

While the countries of East-Central Europe required Western economic assistance during the communist era things were more complicated in the cultural realm. The language barrier did not allow for the full intellectual potential of, say, the Lublin School of Philosophy, to be revealed to the West. Some of its works though, especially by Fr. Prof. Mieczysław Albert Krąpiec, were published in English in the West.

It will be worthwhile to begin a dialogue and an exchange of thoughts within the Catholic circles of Europe, North America and South America as to how lively philosophical thought is in the universities and seminaries. In spite of the collapse of the Soviet Bloc, anti-Christian ideology in different forms and with different philosophical foundations, including liberalism and post-modernism, is still an influential presence.

Marxism is not dead yet. The West succumbs to all sorts of ideologies because it is increasingly weaker intellectually and the mass media and materialism dominate. What is necessary is a dialogue between East and West within the framework of the common heritage of classical philosophy, the only antidote to the pluralism of philosophical errors lying at the root of so many dangerous ideologies. There are still some healthy circles left after all.

An intelligent, educated and righteous Christian humanism faces many difficult challenges. All that is required is a sober mind, a humble heart and social and international solidarity to regain the public sphere, including an influence on culture which is threatened both in the West and in post-communist countries, for Christianity. Just as ideology distorts the end of culture so too mass culture deprives it of any deeper meaning. For, as John Paul II emphasized, man lives a truly human life thanks to culture and culture gives meaning to his existence. This is the role that culture must again play. Since the collision with a false understanding of culture in the former communist countries was much sharper that in the West, it is in those countries that circles exist that see the dangers brought by modern culture, cut off from the past, geared towards hedonism and deprived of Transcendence, with greater clarity. This is why it is important for the West to learn from the experiences of the post-communist countries before they are engulfed by a flood of neo-socialism that could perhaps be even more dangerous than communism itself.

Freedom and Tolerance

The word "tolerance" today is an integral part of our description of western democracy. On the one hand, the word "tolerance" expresses an attitude of being open to the views of others in matters of a world-view and religion. On the other hand it has become a yardstick for whether, or not, a person fits in the world of our time. Intolerance is stigmatized as fundamentalism or even fascism. We may say that without tolerance there would be no democracy today, but the word unfortunately has also become part of the vocabulary of "political correctness".

The term "tolerance" began its career in the seventeenth century. Before that time it appeared in Latin in association with the virtue of fortitude. Apart from its literal meaning, it had a moral meaning. Tolerance was steadfastness. In its most literal sense, it referred to physical endurance. To tolerate something is quite literally to bear something, or bear with something. By analogy it referred to endurance or steadfastness in the face of some evil. Part of the virtue of fortitude is the ability to put up a sustained resistance to evil, and so tolerance is very close to fortitude.

In the seventeenth century, the tolerance (or toleration) was extended to matters of religion and politics. At that time the religious conflicts that arose in the Reformation were still raging and were leading to political battles and even bloody wars. On the twenty-fourth of May in 1689, the British Parliament passed the "Toleration Act" that allowed dissenting Protestants freedom of worship. The act particularly concerned Baptists, Congregationalists, and Methodists. Also in 1689, John Locke published the first volume of his *Epistula de Tolerantia*.[11] Tolerance acquired a religious, philosophical, and political

---

11. When John Locke promoted his principle of tolerance, he left the door open for intolerance toward Catholics, ostensibly for politically reasons rather than on religious grounds.

status, but its most important context was in matters of religion. The "Toleration Act", interestingly enough, did not extend to Catholics. The umbrella of toleration did not protect Catholics. Their religious practices were not tolerated, and they had no place in public life. Religious freedom was not something to be enjoyed by Catholics.

Over time toleration extended beyond religion to the sphere of world-views, until it became the first commandment (the "prime directive") in an ideological sense. Tolerance has today essentially changed the meaning of freedom. Freedom in the classical sense ended where evil begins, and evil was forbidden,[12] but today tolerance sets the boundaries of freedom. Tolerance, however, has its own axiological system, its own system of values, and this is not in complete agreement with the Decalogue or with the classical ethics of natural law, which conforms with the Decalogue.

Today in the west traditional ethics, as upheld by Christianity is more and more in conflict with the ideological principle of tolerance. The perennial ethics for which Christianity has been a vehicle commands us to do good and avoid evil.[13] The ideological principle commands us simply to be tolerant.

"Evil" is neutered in this ideology. Instead of "evil", we are taught to speak of "differences", "diversity", and "minorities". We must be tolerant of anything different. When new laws strike at traditional principles and values, and offend the upright and well-formed conscience, the media is immediately prepared to re-educate us and reshape our attitudes. We are manipulated to speak and think in terms of tolerance instead of in terms of good and evil. This manipulation begins in how we speak of moral matters. From there it extends to the political arena and to civilization as a whole. By changing the way we speak, the media tries to change reality itself. This attitude, that by using certain phrases, we can actually change reality,

---

12. As in the words of the 19th century president of Ecuador, Garcia Moreno: "Freedom for everyone and everything, except for evil and evil-doers".
13. This principle appeared in Cicero. St. Thomas Aquinas referred to it and wrote: "...bonum est faciendum et prosequendum, et malum vitandum", S.Th. I-II, 94, 2. Cf. M. A. Krąpiec, *Person and Natural Law*, Peter Lang, New York 1993.

is in fact a reversion to magic. The west is not merely going back to pre-Christian civilization, but is turning its back on civilization as it looks to barbarism. Before Christianity, Greek and Roman thinkers and lawmakers had worked to refine their ideas of morality, but this heritage is rejected as well.[14] Aristotle had observed more than two thousand years ago that a man without morality is worse than a beast.[15] What can remain of a man's conscience if he can no longer distinguish between good and evil? If he has lost the ability to distinguish, he cannot be accountable for his actions. Is the ethics of our day supposed to be a system designed for people who are held to be morally incompetent? Is it a system designed for the morally insane? What does it mean to be tolerant? The problem of tolerance was raised during the Reformation and it primarily concerned religion. The principle of *cuius regio, eius religio*, was that he who rules a land may also impose his own religion upon his subjects. In the face of this principle, statesmen looked for ways in which people of different religious confessions could coexist, how Catholics could live with Protestants, and *vice versa*. The Edict of Nantes was one of most famous acts of tolerance, and from 1598 to 1685 it granted many rights to the Huguenots in a France that remained officially Catholic. Today, tolerance is more than a question of religion. Tolerance is a panacea for questions of morality, life-style, and world-view. The civilized man is a tolerant man, and he sees people who don't practice his kind of tolerance as primitive fundamentalists. What the word "tolerance" means exactly today is rather vague, because the word has become an ideological slogan. The slogan, in its extreme form, is even a reversal of traditional morality. Tolerance means to do evil and avoid good! How else can we explain why perverts and criminals are protected? How can we explain the invasion of books and films that glorify evil

---

14. The preamble to the Constitution of the European Union omits any mention of Christianity. It appeals to an indescript and general "religious heritage" ("they draw inspiration from the cultural, religious, and humanistic heritage of Europe, a heritage whose values are always present in it and which has rooted in the life of the society of Europe a perception of the central role of the human person and his inviolable and inalienable rights, and also respect for law"). There are many various religions in Europe today, but the identity of Europe after the fall of the Roman Empire was shaped by Christianity.

15. "...if he have not virtue, he is the most unholy and the most savage of animals...", *Politics*, I, 1. 12.

and present blasphemies against Christianity? Tolerance has come to mean the ostracism of those who hold normal moral attitudes. In a more moderate form, tolerance does not urge people to support evil, merely to accept it and consent to it. It makes the good into something relative and subjective. The good becomes merely one of several options, a mere matter of taste. The question of good and evil must be trivialized. Evil may not be condemned or rebuked, and so it is sheltered and strengthened. This is the ethics of the west today. This ethics is based on an ideology that produces a social psychosis through the media and politics. Any public person who dissents from this ideology loses his position in public life. He is stigmatized or becomes a social non-entity. The ideology of tolerance has become one of the most important requirements of "political correctness".

It is interesting that unlike previous ideologies of the twentieth century such as Hitler's Nazism and the Communism of Marx, Lenin, and Stalin, the ideology of tolerance has no single author. While it has binding authority, its authority is not connected with the name of any leader or any founder. It exercises its authority impersonally as a kind of artificially produced social pressure. If someone disagrees with it, he does not know to whom he should direct his objections. Like every ideology, it grows out of something deeper, whether a philosophy or a type of civilization. In fact, political correctness as a tactic was developed by the leftist Frankfurt School. It was a tactic to advance communism by destroying the West from within, specifically by neutralizing those who dared to criticize Marxism. Political correctness was the tactic of changing the way people talk and think, by teaching people that if they express their beliefs they are being disrespectful to others. They must avoid expressing their beliefs to make up for the injustices of the past. The Frankfurt School was founded in 1923 and in 1935 moved from Germany to the USA.

We face a basic ethical question today. We must define the moral principle that will assign the space to a shared civilization that rests upon freedom. Will we choose the ethics of the good or the ethics of tolerance? The ethics of tolerance is a perversion of the ethics of the good. It is a caricature, but it is so cunning that the one ethics may be easily confused with the other. The ethics of tolerance is also a caricature of the virtue of Christian mercy and willingly cloaks itself in that garb.

The ethics of the good is rooted in classical Greek ethics. It is based on the idea that man can objectively recognize the good and choose it. This, however, is difficult in practice, and so people must be properly educated and formed. Each person must be educated and formed to develop his ability to recognize and choose what is good. Christianity explained the weaknesses of human nature in terms of the effects of original sin, and to overcome these effects education is not enough. Supernatural grace is necessary to do good, especially to attain the final end of life. The ethics of the good does not conceal the truth about man and his difficult moral condition. The ethics of tolerance tries to dispense with this truth in the name of humanism. It permits man to do what he pleases without regard to good and evil. The ethics of tolerance undermines our ability to recognize, to recognize and choose objective goods. Good, like religion, is a private matter for the secular post-Protestant state. While the good is a private matter, evil in all its forms is publicly advertised. There is pressure from many sides to live at peace with evil and accept it. This is what is meant by a tolerant man, while someone who does not accept evil is considered to be a fundamentalist.

The ethics of tolerance disguises itself as Christian mercy, but it is no such a thing. Christian mercy understands that someone may find himself in a bad situation but is still capable of willfully rejecting evil.[16] Mercy demands that we climb toward the good. Tolerance accepts evil, and even demands

---

16. "Accordingly the motive of "mercy," being something pertaining to "misery," is, in the first way, anything contrary to the will's natural appetite, namely corruptive or distressing evils, the contrary of which man desires naturally, wherefore the Philosopher says (Rhet. ii, 8) that "pity is sorrow for a visible evil, whether corruptive or distressing." Secondly, such like evils are yet more provocative of pity if they are contrary to deliberate choice, wherefore the Philosopher says (Rhet. ii, 8) that evil excites our pity "when it is the result of an accident, as when something turns out ill, whereas we hoped well of it." Thirdly, they cause yet greater pity, if they are entirely contrary to the will, as when evil befalls a man who has always striven to do well: wherefore the Philosopher says (Rhet. ii, 8) that "we pity most the distress of one who suffers undeservedly.", S.Th. II-II, 30, 1.

that we lower ourselves to its level. These are two different ethics and correspond to two different civilizations. How is it that the ethics of the good and the ethics of tolerance are so easily confused? In both cases, we are dealing with a situation that evokes our pity. Tolerance wears the disguise of mercy, but it is not mercy. The emotion of pity must be filtered through the reason first if we are to know if it is inclined to virtue or vice. This will depend on our rational attitude toward evil.[17] When people promote tolerance as a basic principle of action they appeal to the emotions but not to reason in an effort to evoke pity. People are led to think in this way: the poor murderer who must sit for so many years in isolation without his family; the poor deviant, the poor thief with no family or friends, unable to come and go as he wishes. Criminals are transformed into victims by evoking feelings of pity, where this logic leads to the difference between reprehensible and responsible behavior being erased. When the feeling of mercy prevails over our ability to make rational judgments and over our ability to recognize causes and effects, mercy is quickly transformed into its opposite. Instead of healing evil, we leave it untouched, and so evil can proliferate.

Another danger is that people will confuse their feelings with their conscience. Conscience is an act of rational judgment![18] The feeling of mercy is not that of conscience. Conscience is an act of reason. The ideology of tolerance aims to eliminate the role of the reason in moral judgment. Reason will be cut off from reality because good is seen as relative and subjective. It will be cut off from the area of conscience because the emotions are considered important, and pity is the most important. When the reason is disengaged, people are easy victims for manipulation.

What are the practical consequences when the ethics of tolerance are dominant in particular areas of man's moral life?

---

17. "Mercy signifies grief for another's distress. Now this grief may denote, in one way, a movement of the sensitive appetite, in which case mercy is not a virtue but a passion; whereas, in another way, it may denote a movement of the intellective appetite, in as much as one person's evil is displeasing to another.", S.Th., II-II, 30, 3.
18. "...for conscience may be resolved into *cum alio scientia* [that is knowledge applied to an individual case].", S.Th., I, 79, 13.

Ethics concern the moral life of the individual. The good we should seek is not an abstraction or value. It is the concrete aim of our natural inclinations. When we speak of the three basic inclinations of our nature we may speak as well of three ends and goods: the preservation of our life, the transmission of life, and our development as persons in the truth. The ethics of the good orders us to do good. This is the source of the imperative that we should respect human life from conception to natural death. We should also be solicitous of man's spiritual development, and so we should work for truth in the media, in politics, and in schools. The ethics of tolerance, on the other hand, promotes suicide and euthanasia as an easy way to resolve the drama of human suffering. It promotes abortion as a way of ridding ourselves of unwanted children. It has no qualms about the use of deception and manipulation in public life, when this suits its aims.

In the economic order, the family is the focus of traditional economy. The child comes into the world and develops in a family. His family protects his material existence and fosters his spiritual growth. The ethics of tolerance promotes alternative models of the "family": the single parent, two adults of the same gender, alternative ways of bringing children into the world such as *in vitro* fertilization, often where the biological parents do not have any personal connection. The promotion and legalization of "homosexual marriages" results from the application of the principles of the ethics of tolerance. The countries of the European Union are more and more intensely moving in this direction. There is a similar movement in North America, most notably in Canada.

In the political order, according to the ethics of the good, the political community is based on the foundation of justice, and there are three kinds of justice: commutative, legal, and distributive. Commutative justice concerns relations between individuals. Legal justice concerns itself with the relations between individuals and the society or state. Distributive justice concerns itself with the relations between the society or state and individuals. The classical idea of social justice is complex, for social life is complex. The perfection of society requires that these three types of justice should go together. Meanwhile, in the ethics of tolerance we are dealing with reductionism. It accepts only one kind of justice and the others do not exist or are regarded as unimportant. It is guided by the principle of the strong prevailing over the weak, whether it is the stronger individual, corporation, or state. In this way the deepest meaning of social life is destroyed. Commutative justice concerns only the partners in their business agreements but does not concern the nature of their business.

Legal justice is abused to promote economic environments connected with the circles of power. Distributive justice makes it possible to treat the state as the fiefdom of certain interest groups. Such a system is sick and these are illusions of justice.

In the relation between politics and justice there is the danger that the most important aim of politics will be denied. Justice demands that we give to each what is due (*cuique suum*), but justice is inadequate when we think of what we each owe to our parents, what we have inherited from those who have gone before, and God. Yet our parents, our predecessors, and God are at the foundations of our social existence. God is the transcendental reason and the cause of causes. Yet we see that these points of reference are denied in the west, especially now in the European Union. Not only is the role of the family and of parents undermined, the entire heritage of Europe is being rejected. Finally, society is shutting its gates to God. The rights of children are increased while the rights of parents are diminished. Since the state is the source of laws and rights, children are more and more the property or wards of the state. Experiments with the preamble to the constitution show how the authors are trying to forget the two millennia of Christianity that essentially shaped the identity of Europe. In the absence of God, the whole legal and moral order drifts like a leaf in the wind, and the only remaining right is the right of the strongest concealed in legalism. The proposed constitution of the European Union refers neither to Christianity nor to God.

The ethics of tolerance is a fusion of two ideologies, liberalism and socialism. Liberalism is individualism. It treats our moral judgments as relative and individual. Morality and religion become private matters. Socialism, on the other hand, is the ideology of the group. Liberalism with its proclaimed glorification of individual rights is only a starting point. In fact, liberalism is swallowed up by socialism. Hobbes and Locke taught that the individual freely relinquishes his natural rights to the political authorities. The state in which the individual lives is in fact a socialist state. The state is superior to the individual.

The political authorities determine the law and how the law is interpreted. The slogan of tolerance is a tool for destroying the individual's ability to understand reality in terms of good and evil, and so he can no longer react properly to good and evil. When our understanding is dimmed, the media can easily manipulate our social reactions for or against anything with no regard to good and evil. Tolerance is a way of manipulating society.

When we refer to tolerance in our moral judgments we are eroding the ground we stand on for we are losing contact with reality and reason. The fundamental moral question is whether man is capable of objectively recognizing good and evil, and whether by recognising them he can take a proper stand toward them, which would then lead to making the right choice. The traditional western ethics of the good is based on a positive answer to these questions. Man can recognize objective good and evil, he can take a proper stand, and it is in his power to make the right choice. The ethics of tolerance answers in the negative: man cannot know objective good and evil, his beliefs are a private matter; choice is good because it is choice, not because it aims at the objective good.

The ethics of tolerance is the foundation of post-modern ethics. Postmodern ethics gather together most of the destructive philosophical positions in western philosophy which it lie at the base of contemporary European culture. Post-modernism is postliberalism and post-socialism. It has an aversion to our western heritage, especially Christianity. All the more

142

as Christians we must work to save the ethics of the good, if morality is to be truly morality, and freedom is to be truly freedom. We must recognize true tolerance, which has persons and the good of persons as its object, and never confuse it with indifference, which is only a step away from hatred towards our neighbor.[19]

---

19. "…Then as now, true Christians practiced this tolerance with regard to persons, which is quite simply an evangelical virtue. We must guard ourselves from confusing true tolerance with false tolerance. Is it a question of error? We must combat it with all our forces under whatever form it presents itself, just as it is our duty to combat evil everywhere that we find it. Man would abdicate his quality of being intelligent and moral if he were to act otherwise. Tolerance can only concern itself with persons and it consists in acting with kindness as we act toward equals. There is more, dear sirs, because after having determined the object of this virtue, it is important to define the motive. To be true, tolerance must be based on the feeling of charity and not on indifference in matters of belief or of religion. Many people imagine themselves to be tolerant. They are merely indifferent, which is not at all the same thing. Tolerance does not at all consist in being completely unconcerned about our neighbour under the pretext that we must leave to each his liberty to believe as he wishes. It does not concern in avoiding meddling even if it means his loss. You say you possess the truth, and you will not use all legitimate means to assure its benefits to your equals? You will not look to free them from their errors because you do not want to disturb their liberty of thought and action? You would leave them to run with merry hearts before a certain danger without enlightening them about the consequences of their acts? And you will call this exercising tolerance? But my dear sirs, that would be the most culpable indifference. True tolerance is always accompanied by zeal because it draws from charity the motives that inspire it.", Msgr. Freppel, *Saint Cyprian*, 1873, 2nd edition, pp. 17-19, Bray et Retaux, France.